My First Words

Bilingual
English-Norwegian

BOOK#2

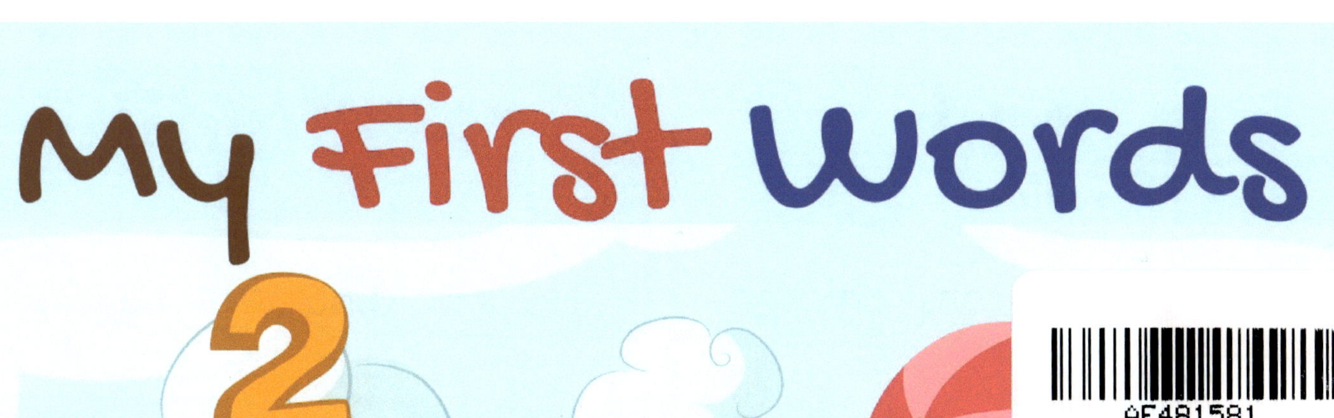

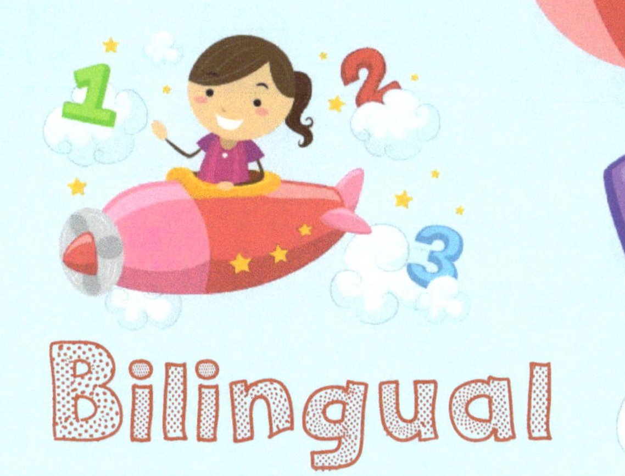

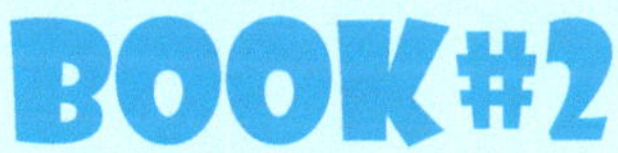

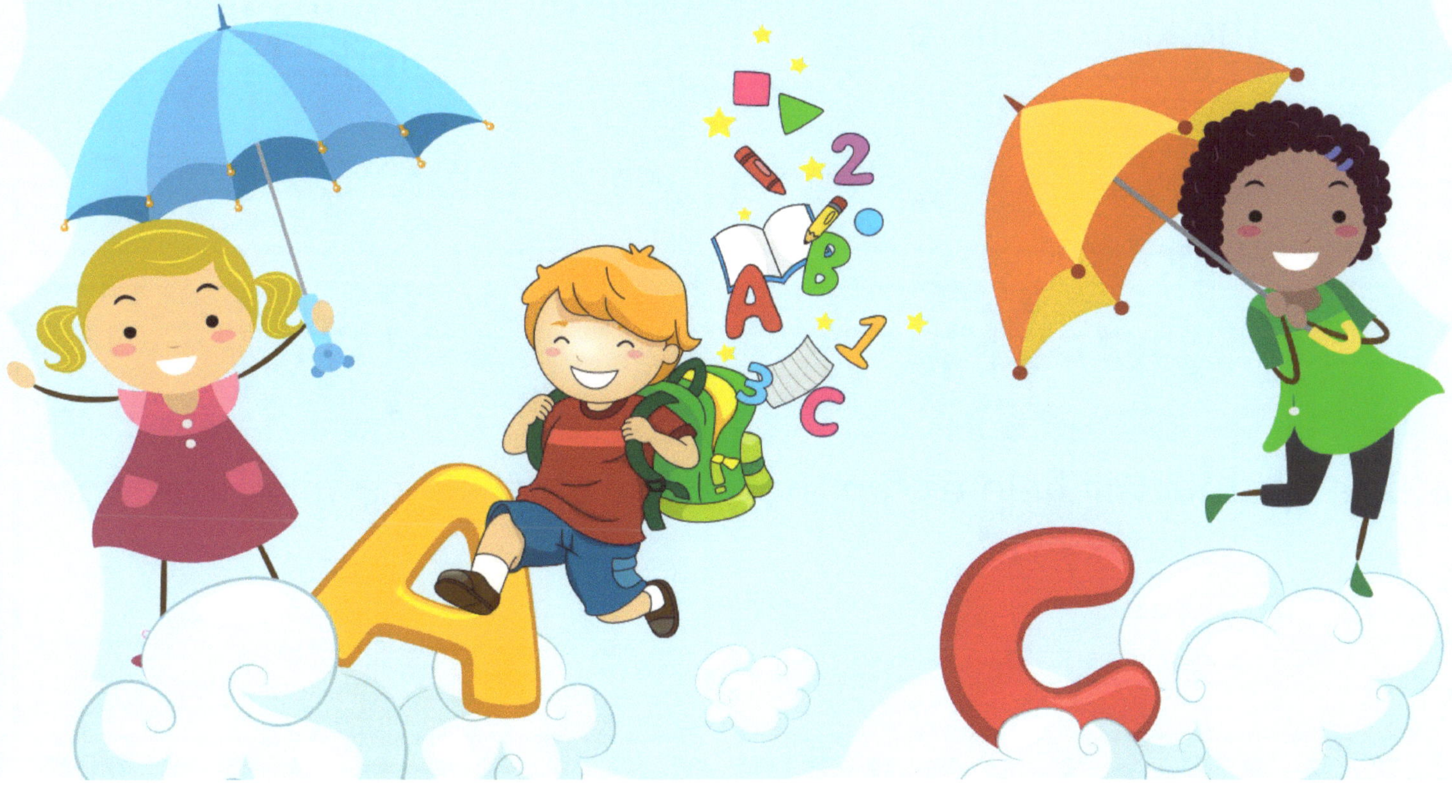

roast

steke

The chef made roast chicken.

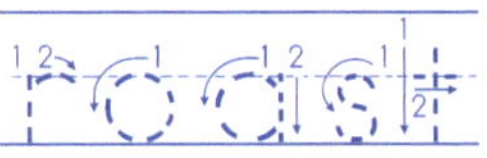

rolling pin

kjevle

He is holding a rolling pin.

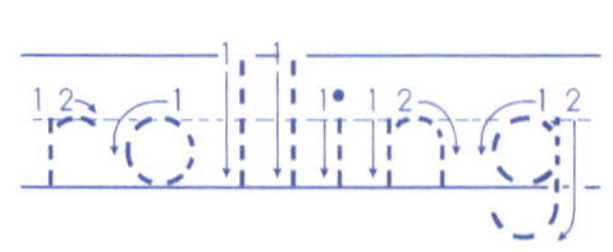

scramble

scramble

My mom is making scrambled eggs for breakfast.

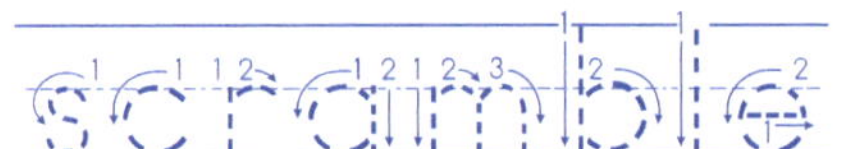

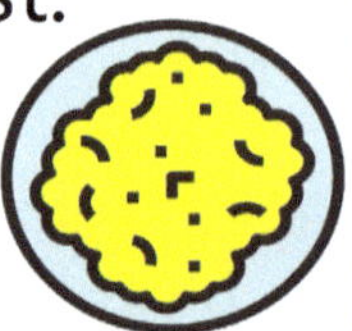

simmer

småkoke

The simmer is rice today.

knife

kniv

The knife is sharp.

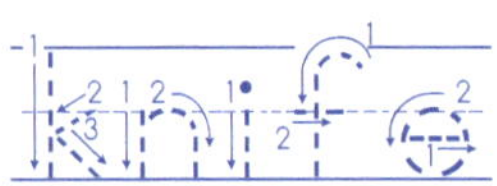

spoon

skje

I eat my food with a spoon and fork.

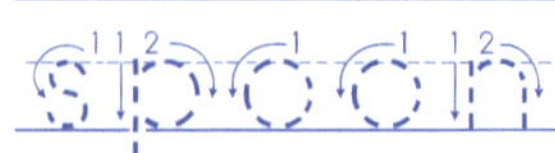

spatula

stekespade

The spatula will help us flip the steak over.

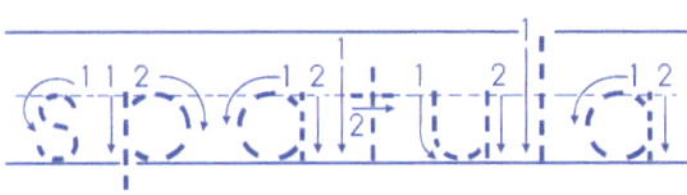

steam

damp

The steam is coming from the pot.

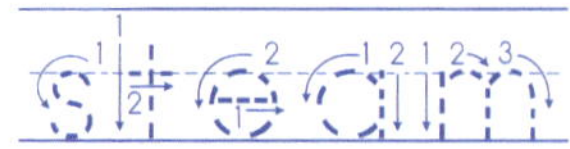

strainer

sil

The strainer is used to strain stuff.

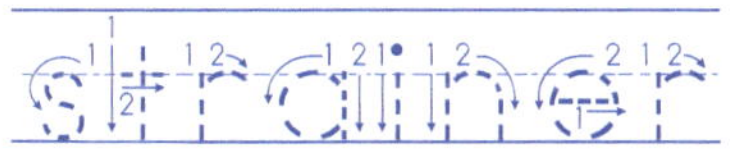 

timer

tidsur

I set my timer for 12:00.

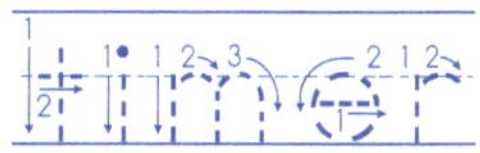 

fork

gaffel

I have lots of metallic forks.

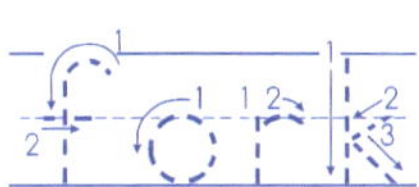 

toaster

Brødrister

The toaster will toast my bread.

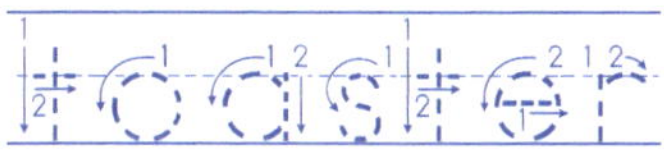 

kettle

Kjele

The kettle has tea inside.

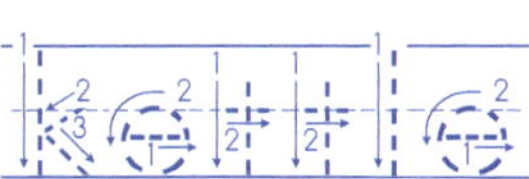 

refrigerator

Kjøleskap

The refrigerator has lots of things inside.

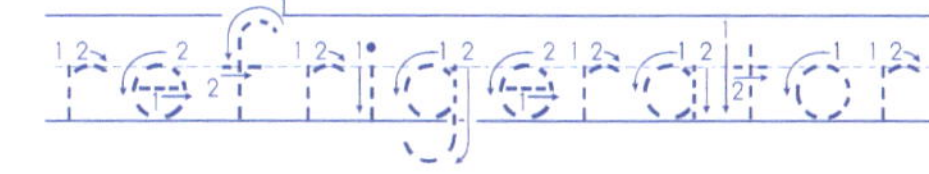 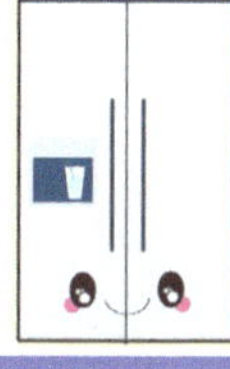

blender

Blender

The blender will mix up my fruits.

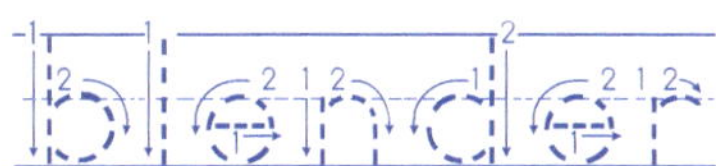 

cabinet

skap

The cabinet has my paper inside.

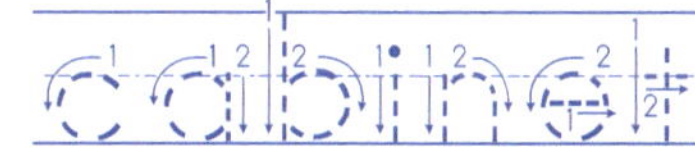 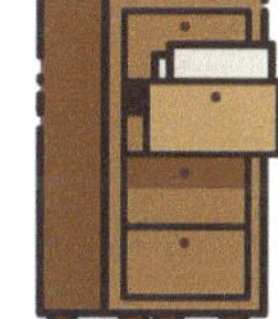

cupboard

Skap

The cupboard has lots of books.

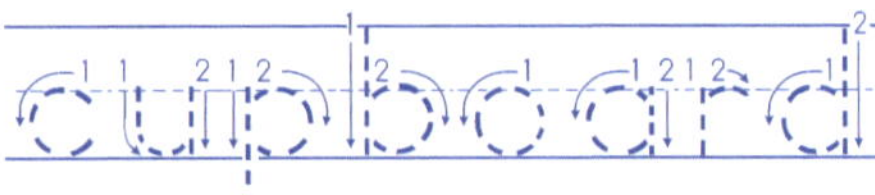 

microwave

mikrobølgeovn

The microwave will heat my food.

back

tilbake

She has a slender back.

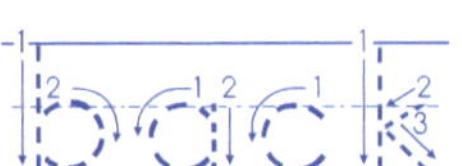 

cheeks

kinn

She kisses her mom on the cheek.

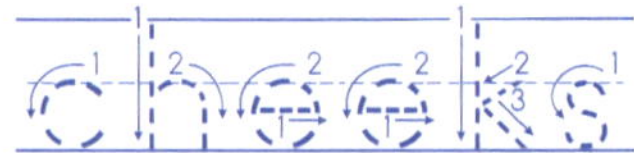 

chest

bryst

The armor is for your chest.

chin

hake

This is my chin!

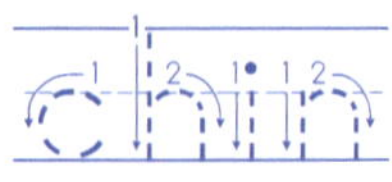 

ears

ører

The ear is hearing something.

 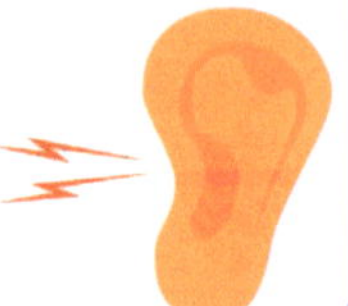

eyebrows

øyenbrynene

The eyebrows are raised.

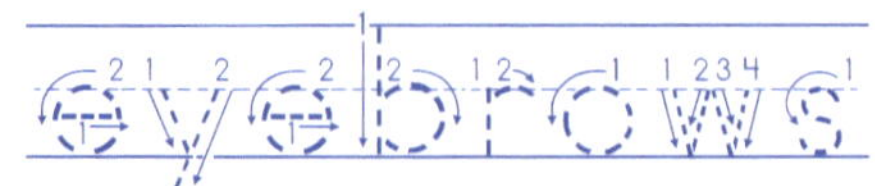 

eyes

øyne

The eyes are blue.

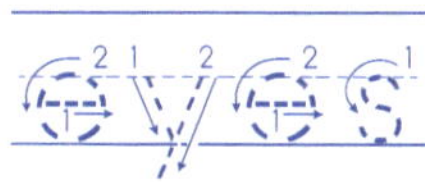

feet

føtter

I have one pair of feet.

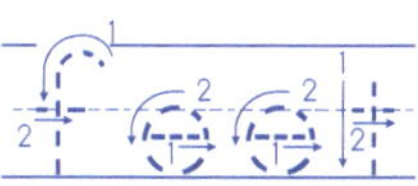

fingers

fingre

The fingers are waving at us.

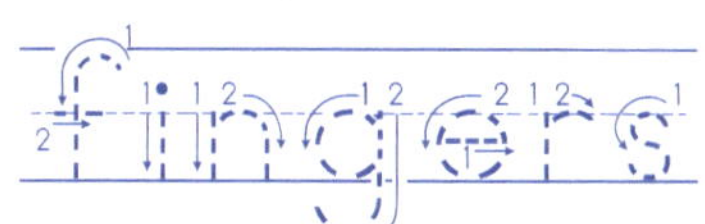

foot

fot

My foot has five fingers.

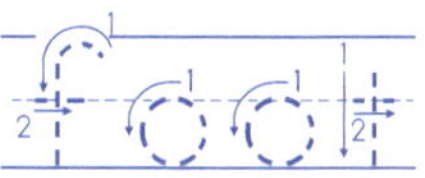

forehead

panne

My brain is behind my forehead.

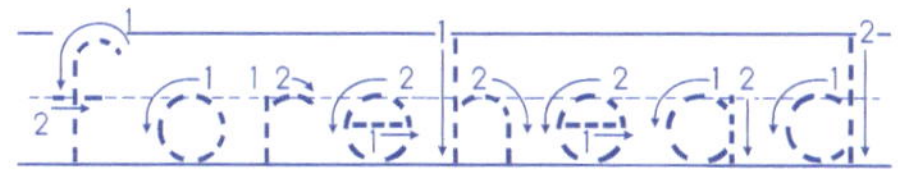

hair

hår

My hair is long and black.

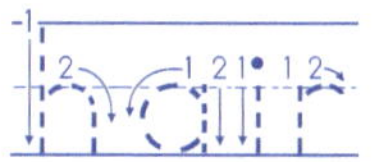

hands

hender

I will wash my hands in the sink.

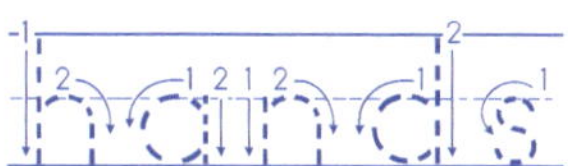

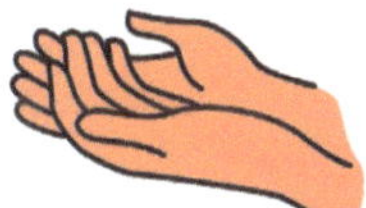

head

hode

She has a big head.

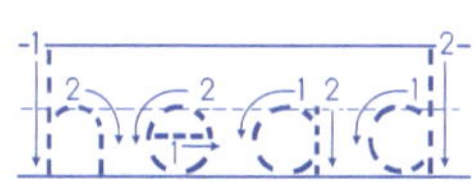

hips
hofter

The gorilla has his hands on his hips.

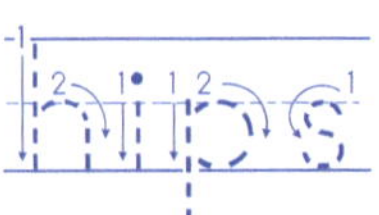

knees
knær

She is begging on her knees.

legs
ben

The tiger has strong legs.

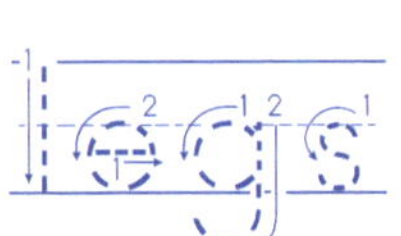

lips
lepper

The lips have lipstick on.

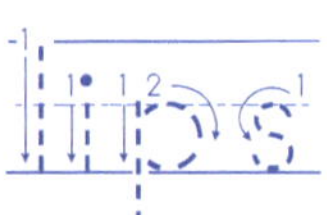

mouth
munn

He is covering his mouth with his hand.

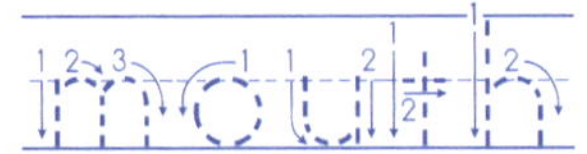

neck
nakke

The necklace is very special to me.

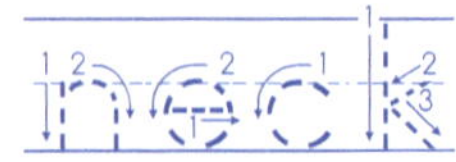

nose
nese

The nose smells something.

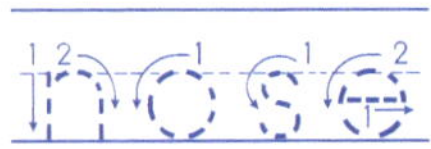

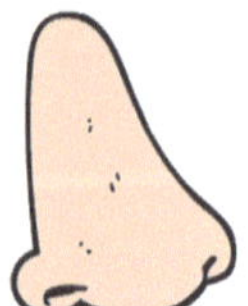

shoulders
skuldre

He puts his hands on his shoulders.

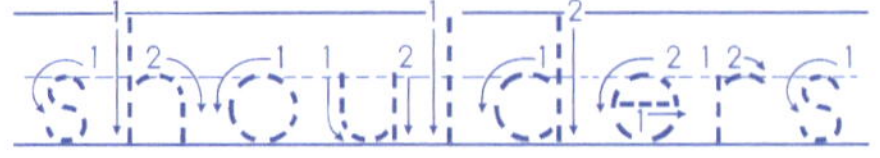

stomach

mage

He has a big stomach.

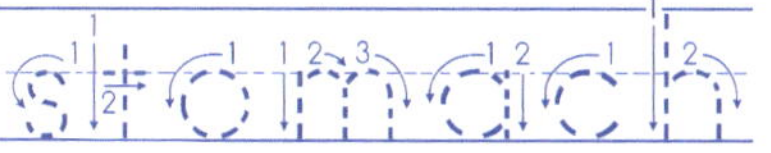 

teeth

tenner

The teeth are clean and white.

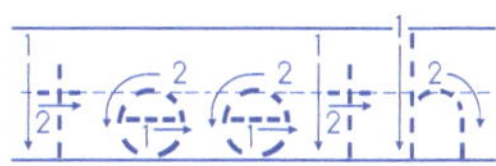 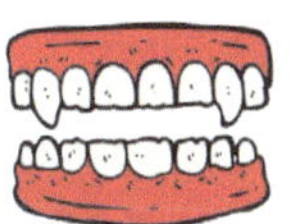

throat

hals

He has a sore throat today.

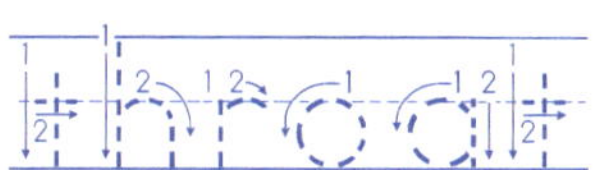 

toes

tær

My toes are small.

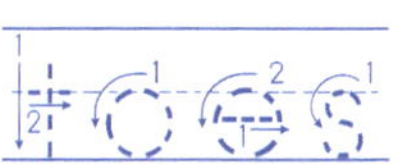 

tongue

tunge

My tongue is licking icecream.

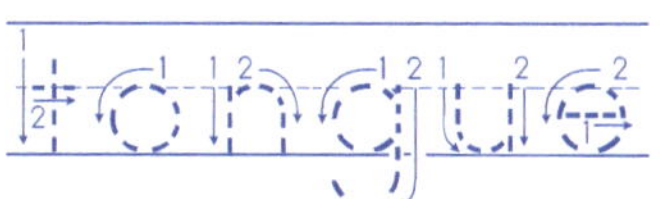 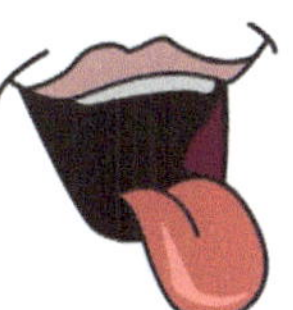

tooth

tann

The tooth has big eyes.

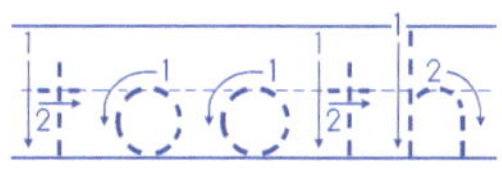 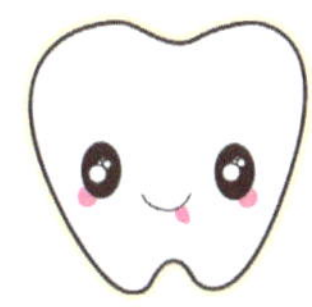

waist

midje

He has his hands on his waist.

overalls

kjeledress

I bought these overalls for you!

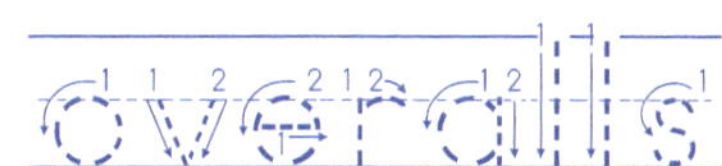 

mittens

votter

The mittens are warm.

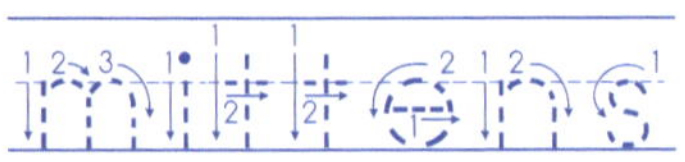 

beanie

Beanie

The beanie is for winter.

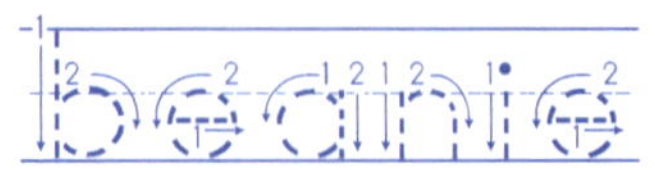 

apron

forkle

I wear my apron when I bake.

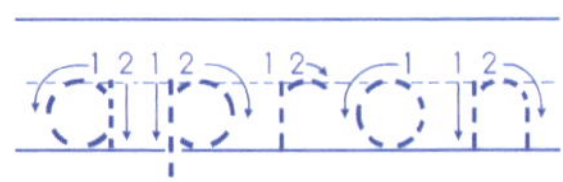 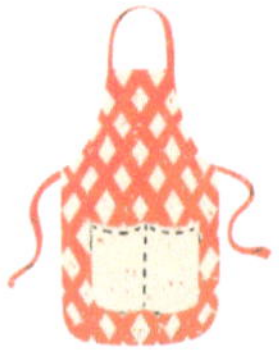

doll

Dukke

The doll is for my baby sister.

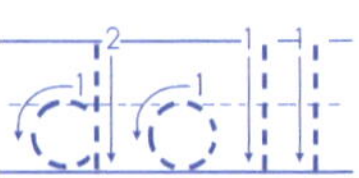 

rattle

rangler

The rattle is for the baby.

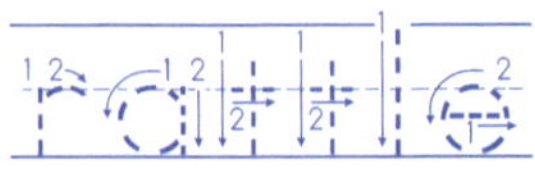 

toy

Leketøy

The toy is entertaining.

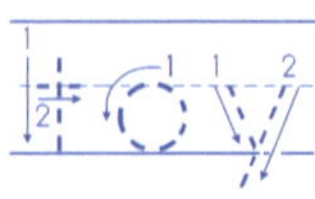 

diaper

Bleie

The baby has to wear a diaper.

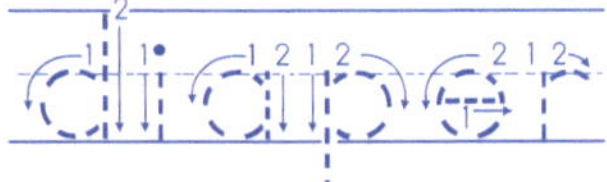 

bassinet

bassinet

She is sleeping in her bassinet.

bib

Smekke

My baby brother has to wear his bib when he is eating.

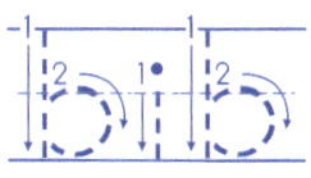

octagon

Octagon

The octagon is saying okay!

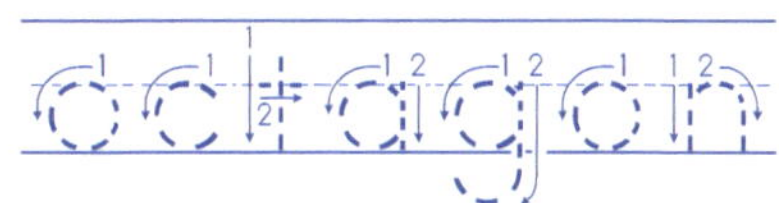

triangle

Triangel

The triangle has three corners.

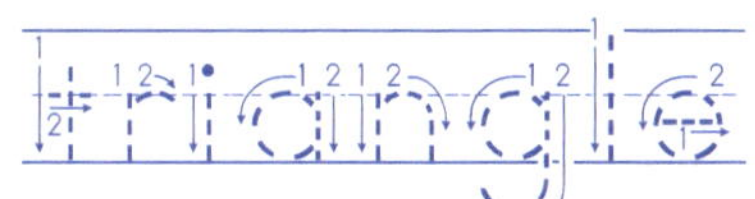

square

Torget

The square has four sides.

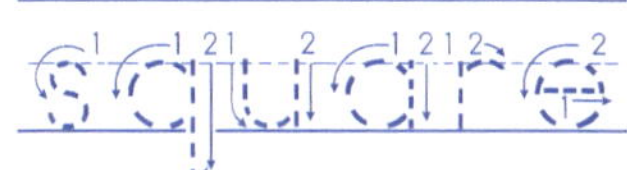

Square

circle

Sirkel

The circle is round.

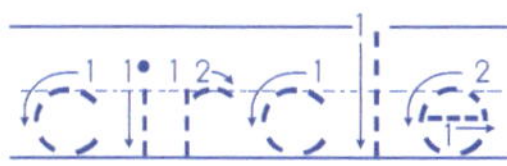
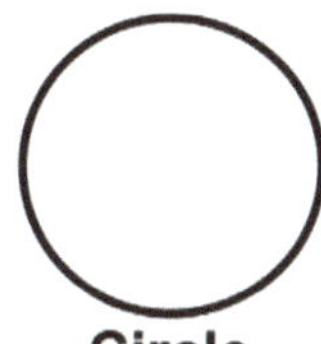

Circle

oval

Oval

The oval looks like a circle.

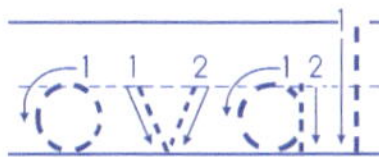
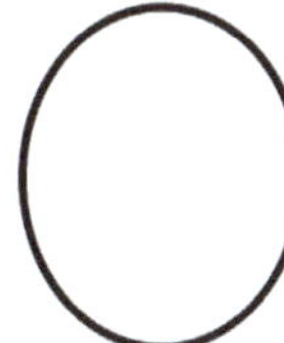

heart

Hjerte

I drew a heart on my paper.

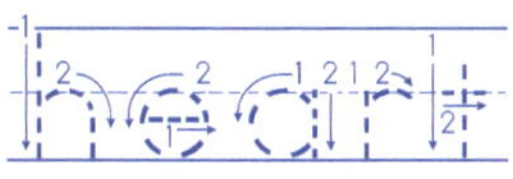

cross

Kryss

That sign is across.

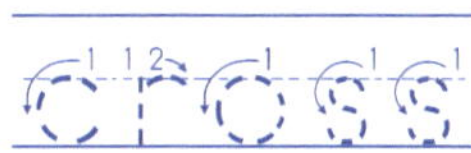
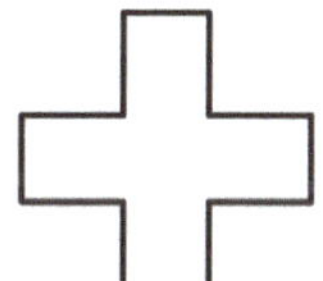

arrow

Pil

The arrow is pointing this way.

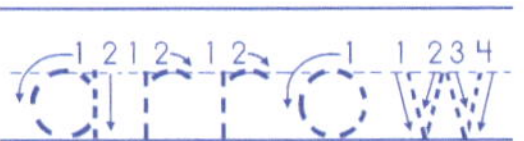
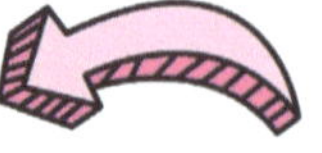

cube

Cube

The cube is 3D.

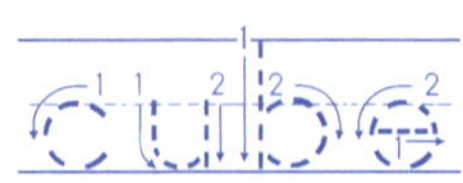
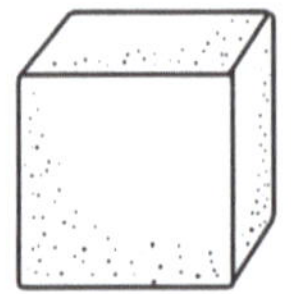

star

Stjerne

The star is yellow and shiny.

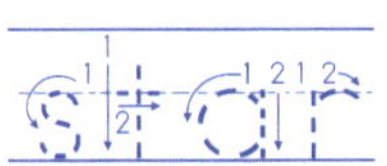

archery

bueskyting

The archery is where you aim.

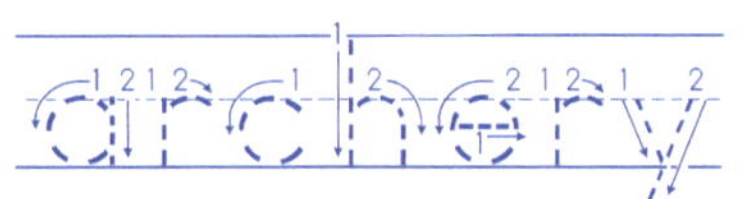

badminton

badminton

My favorite sport is badminton.

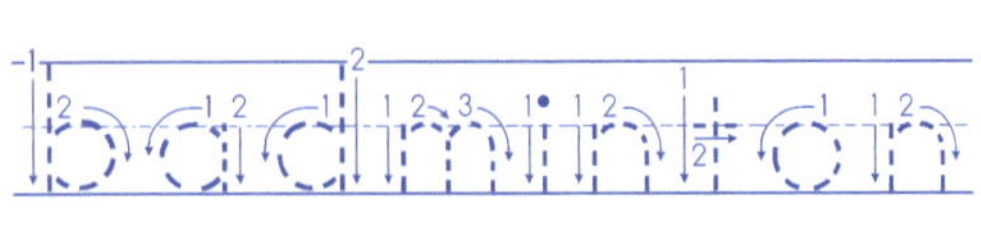

cricket

Siriss

I am very good at cricket.

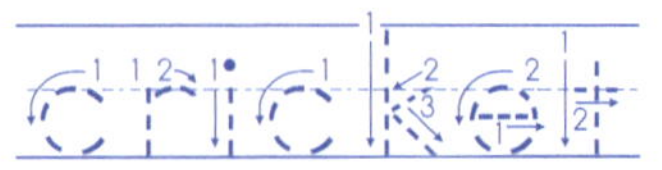

bowling

Bowling

I got one pin down at bowling!

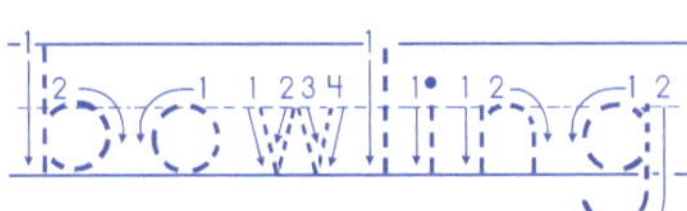

boxing

Boksing

The boxing gloves are hot.

tennis

Tennis

He can hit the ball in tennis.

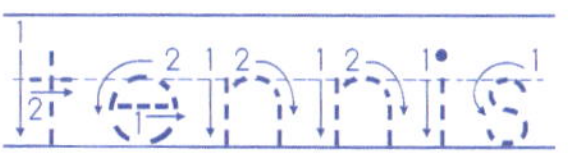 

skateboarding

Rullebrettkjøring

He skateboards all the way to school.

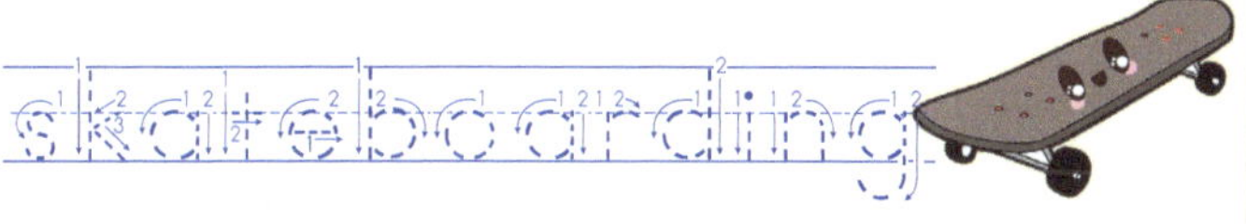

surfing

surfboarding

The shark loves surfing in the ocean.

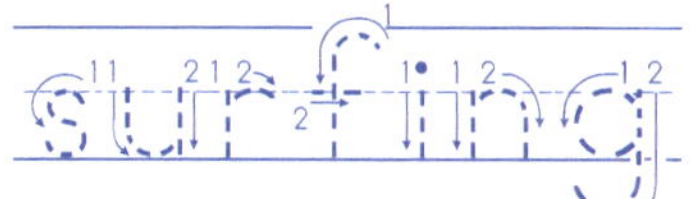 

hockey

hockey

I like to play Ice hockey.

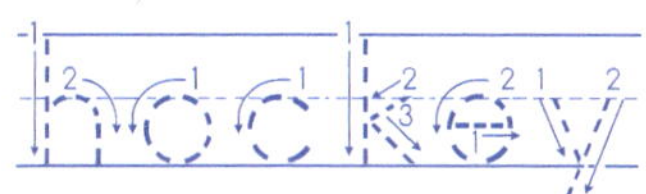 

yoga

yoga

He is closing his eyes and doing yoga.

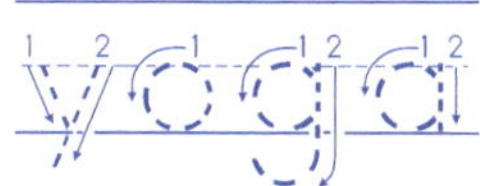

fencing

sverdkamper

They are fencing and dueling together.

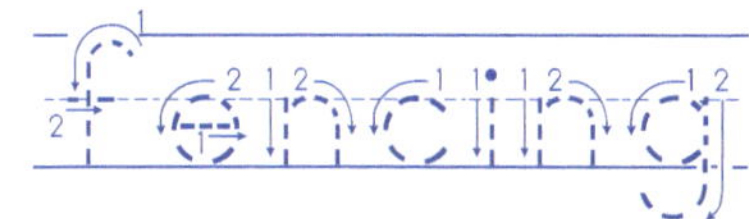 

fitness

Fitness

She will do some fitness in the pool.

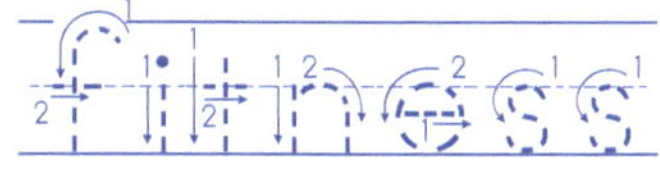 

gymnastics

Gymnastikk

He can do brilliant gymnastics.

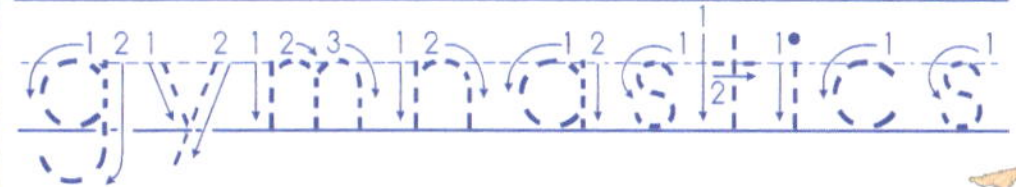 

karate

karate

She is good at kicking in Karate.

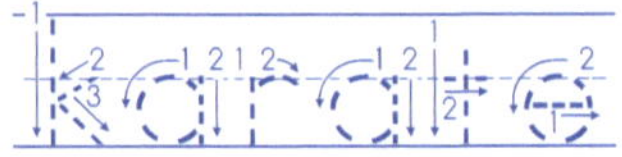

volleyball

volleyball

She is holding a volleyball.

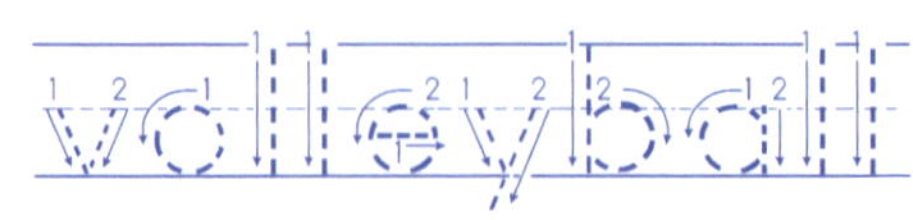

weightlifting

Vektløfting

The girl with brown hair can do weightlifting.

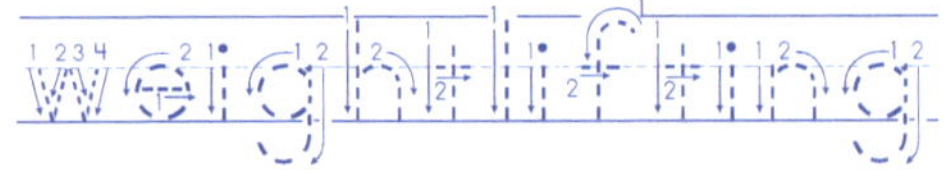

basketball

basketball

He can balance the ball with one finger in basketball.

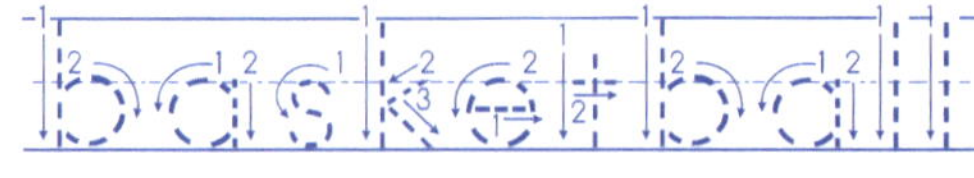

baseball

Baseball

The little chick is in the finales at baseball.

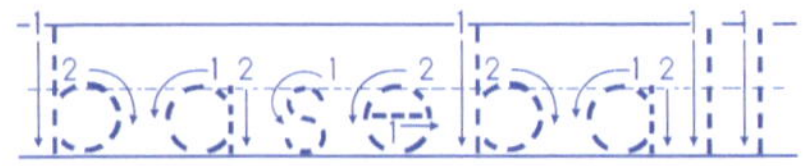

rugby

Rugby

The rugby ball has white stripes.

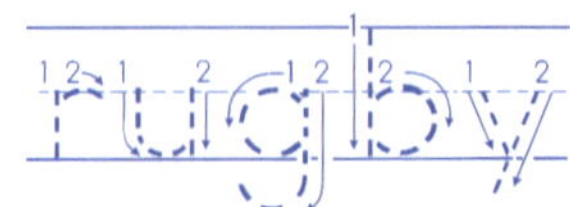

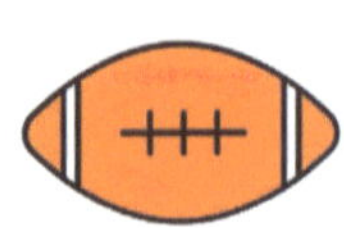

wrestling

bryting

The sumo will compete in wrestling.

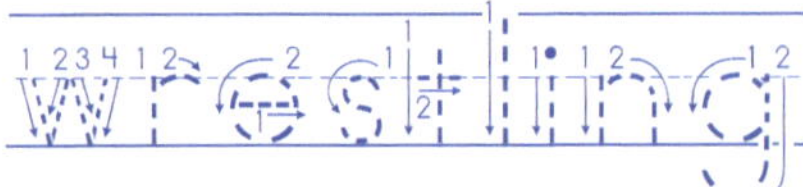

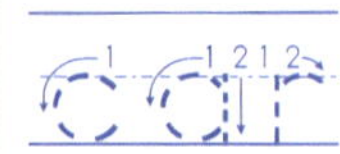

car racing

Billøp

He is number one for car racing.

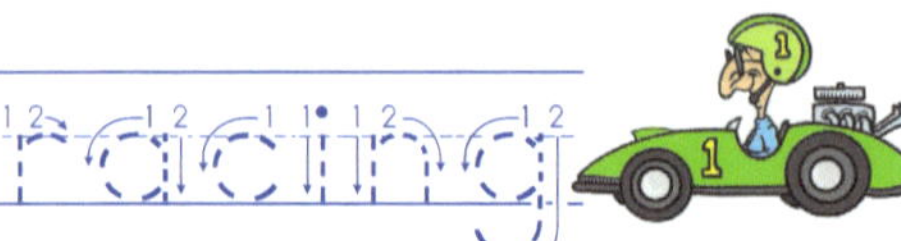

cycling

Sykling

He is peacefully cycling on the road.

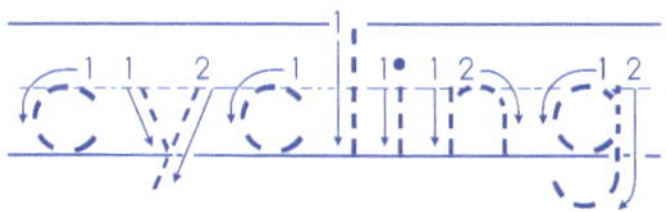 

running

Løping

He is running while listening to his earphones.

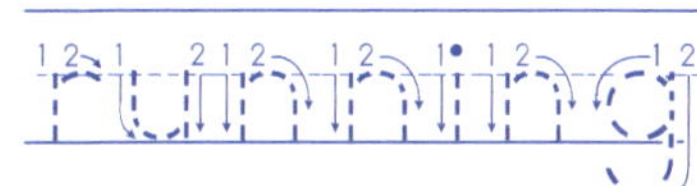 

table tennis

Bordtennis

My brother and dad will play table tennis.

 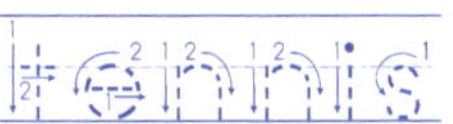 

fishing

fiske

He will go to the river to fish.

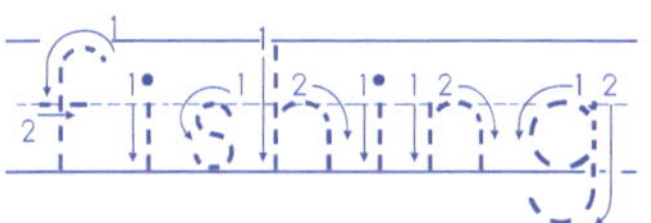 

judo

judo

She has a red belt in Judo.

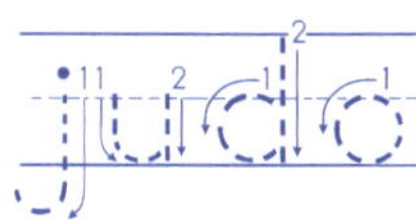 

climbing

klatring

He will climb the ladder.

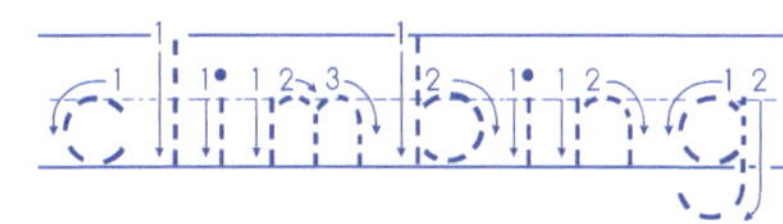 

shooting

skyting

He is shooting the archery board.

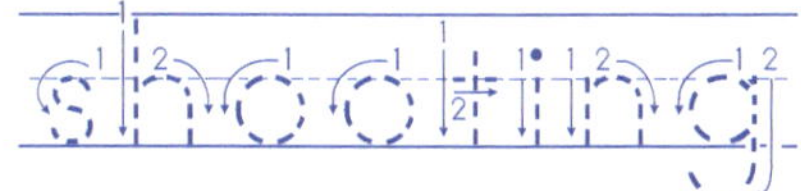 

golf

Golf

She is going to compete in the golf competition.

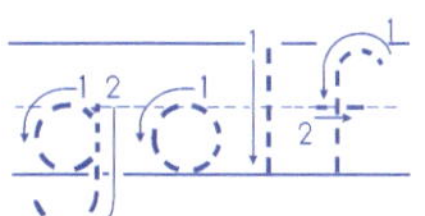

ride

Ri

He will ride his scooter.

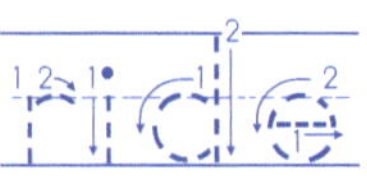

sit down

Sitt ned

They are sitting down together.

stand up

Stå opp

She likes to stand up.

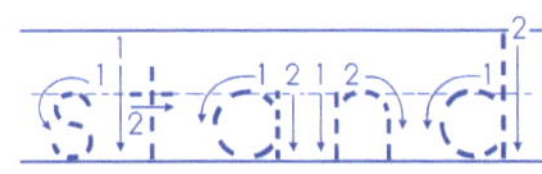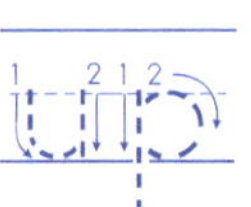

fight

Slåss

They are fighting over the book.

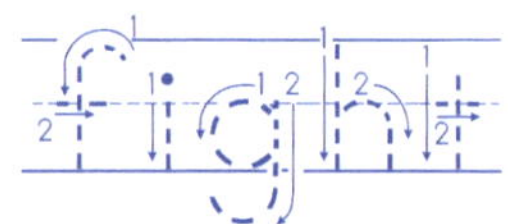

laugh

Latter

He is laughing so hard!

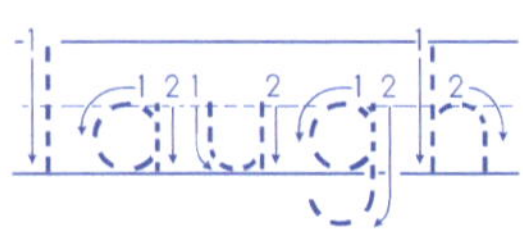

read

Lese

She read a picture book.

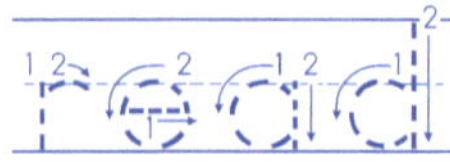

play

Spille

He went to play on the slide.

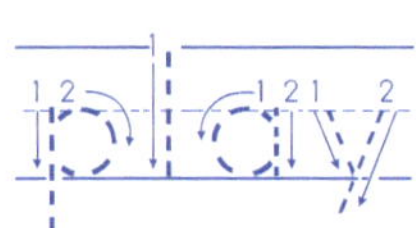

listen

Lytte

He listened for the ice cream cart.

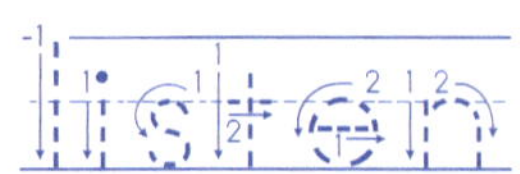

cry
Gråte

He cried because he got a bad grade.

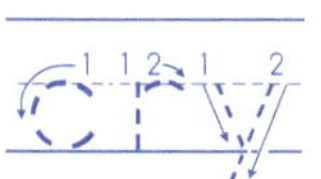

think
Synes at

He thought that the test would be hard.

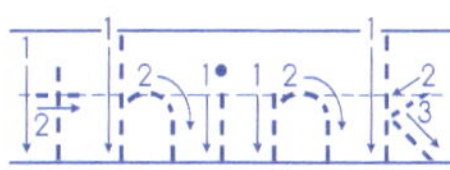

sing
Synge

He sang for the concert.

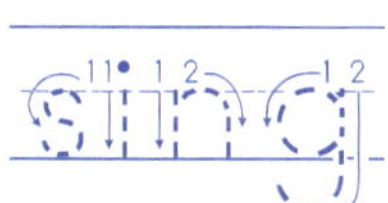

watch tv
Se på TV

He watched TV the whole night.

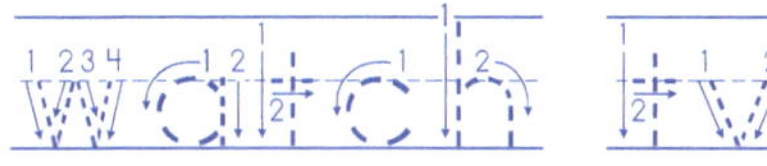

dance
Danse

She was a good dancer.

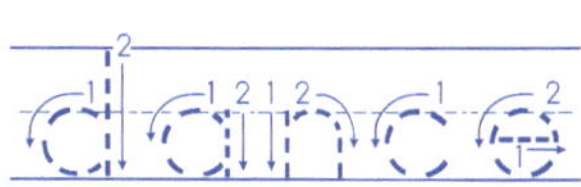

turn on
Slå på

The light is turned on.

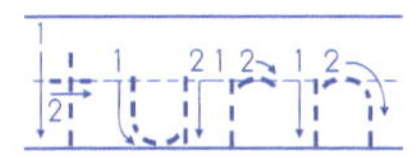
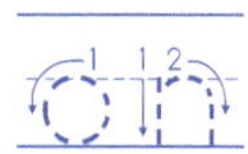

turn off
Skru av

The light is turned off.

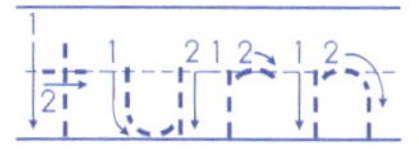
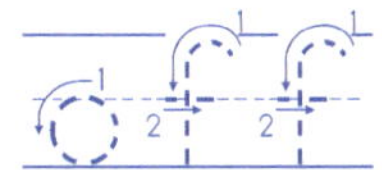

win
Vinne

He won the contest.

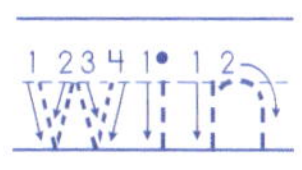

fly
Fly

The parrot can fly.

cut
Kutte opp

He was cutting his nails.

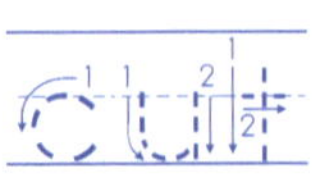

throw away
Kast

He threw away the garbage.

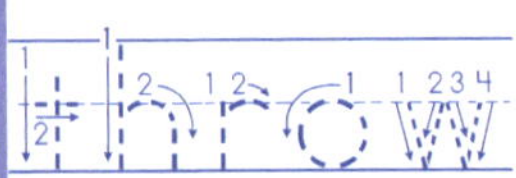

sleep
Sove

He slept soundly.

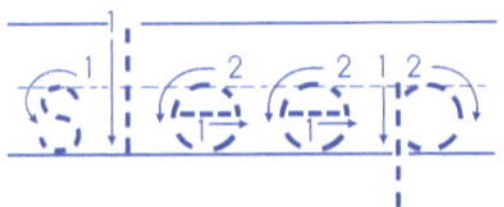

close
Lukk

He closed his mouth shut.

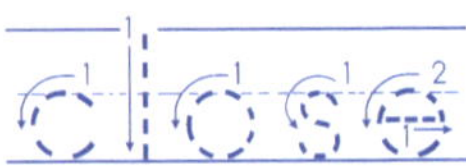

open
Åpen

She opened the bathroom door.

write
Skrive

She wrote with a pencil.

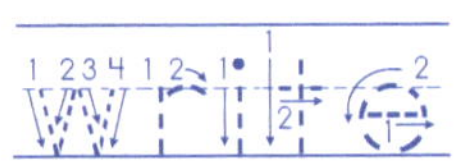

give
Gi

Santa gave her a present.

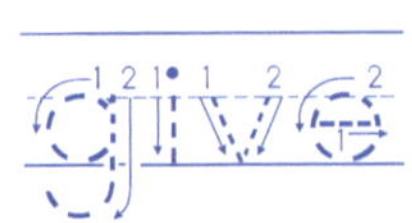

jump

Hoppe

She had fun jumping.

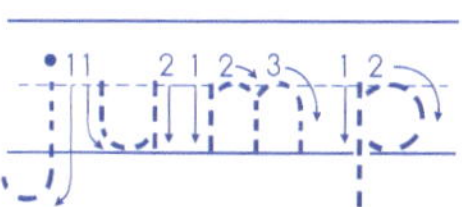

eat

Spise

The shark ate yummy ice cream.

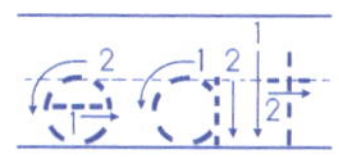

drink

Drikke

The old British man drank tea.

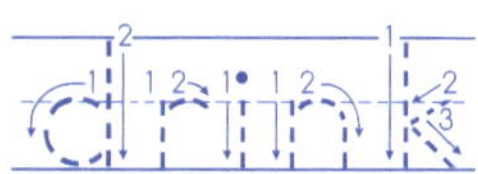

cook

kokk

The microwave cooked his soup.

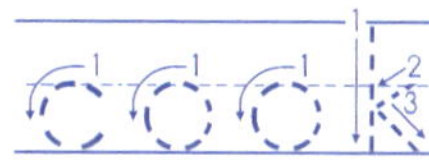

wash

Vask

You need to remember to wash your hands.

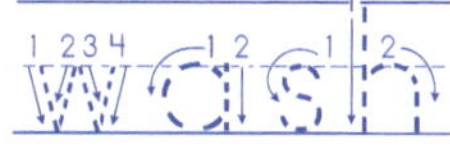

wait

Vente

He was waiting for the bus.

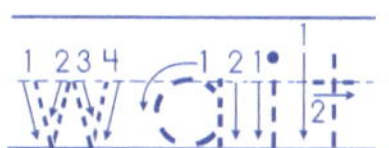

climb

Klatre

She climbed a lot of mountains.

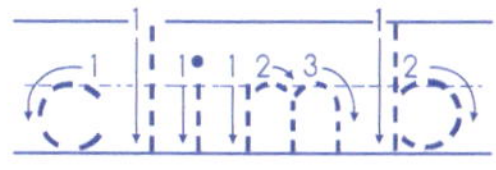

talk

Snakke

Two best friends were talking together.

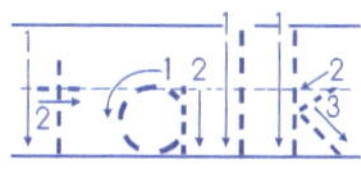

crawl

Crawl

The baby crawled on the floor.

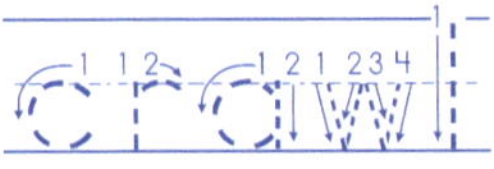

dream

Drøm

The Sloth dreamed about eating leaves.

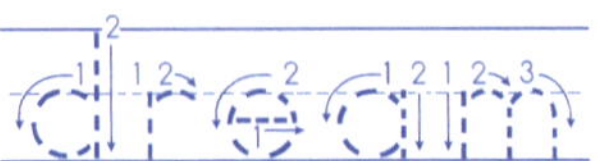

dig

Grave

That strong man dug a swimming pool.

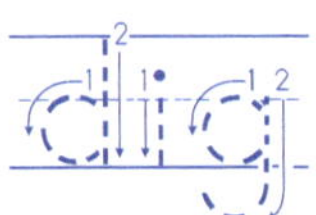

clap

Klapp

The baby clapped her hands.

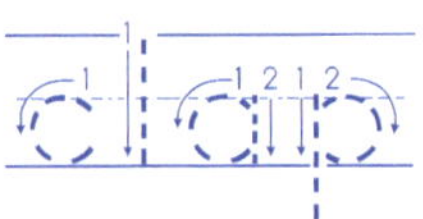

knit

Strikke

She knits with the purple string.

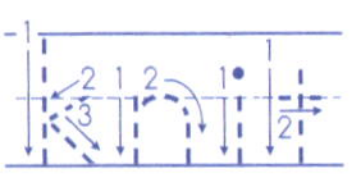

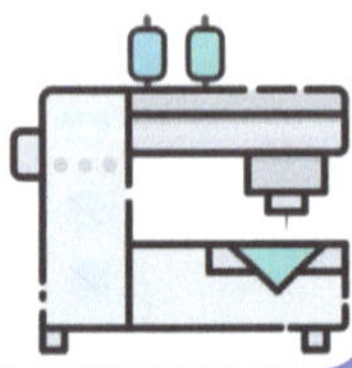

sew

Sy

That is a sewing machine.

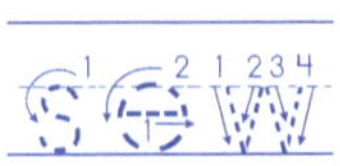

smell

Lukt

The perfume smelled great.

kiss

Kysse

He kissed his mother.

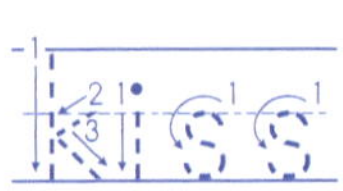

hug
Klem

They hugged each other.

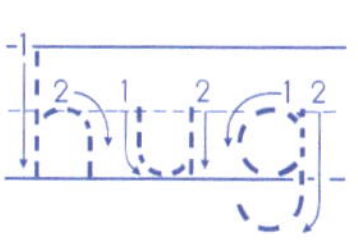

snore
Snorke

The tiger snored.

bathe
Bade

He took a bath.

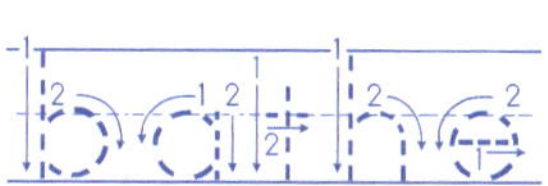

bow
bukker

He bowed to the judge.

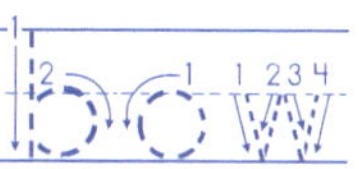

paint
Maling

He painted a colorful picture.

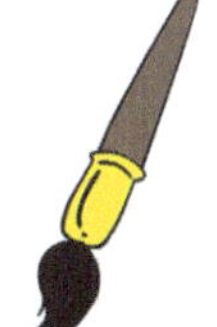

dive
Stupe

He dove to the deepest part of the ocean.

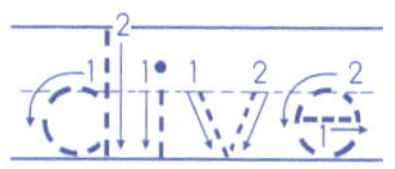

ski
Ski

The ski was expensive.

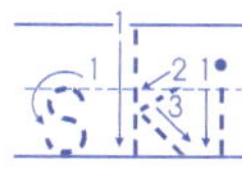

stack
Stable

The books are stacked high.

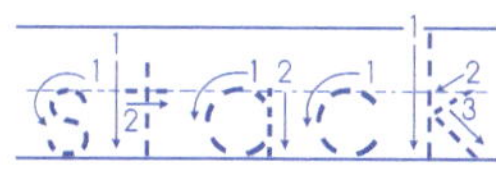

buy

Kjøpe

They bought cereal.

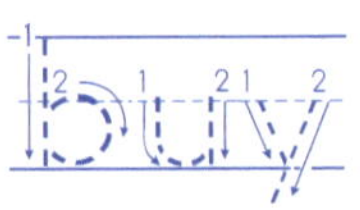 

shake

Riste

They shook hands together.

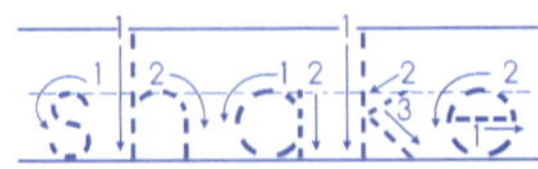 

programmer

Programmerer

He was a smart computer programmer.

veterinarian

Veterinær

She is a veterinarian.

street vendor

gate selger

That street vendor sells hot dogs.

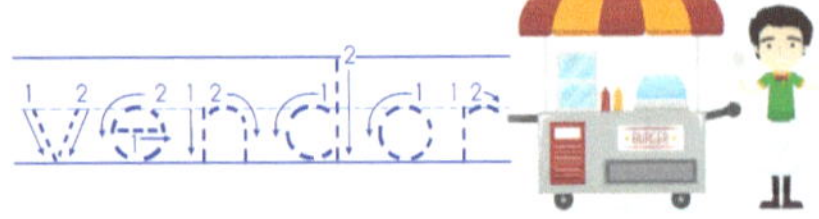 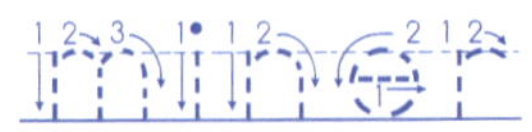 

miner

Gruvearbeider

That Miner will find gold.

teacher

Lærer

The owl is the teacher.

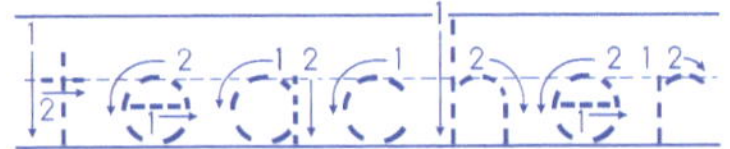 

bellboy

bellboy

That Bellboy is fat.

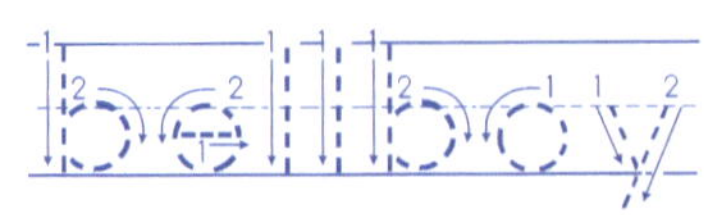 

speaker

Høyttaler

The chicken is a great Speaker.

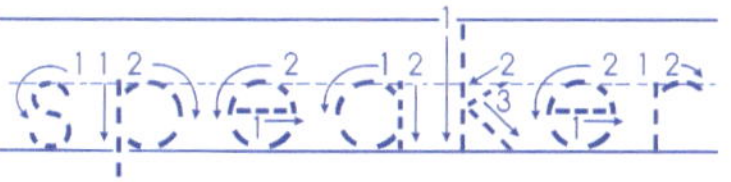 

butcher

Slakter

The Butcher sells fish.

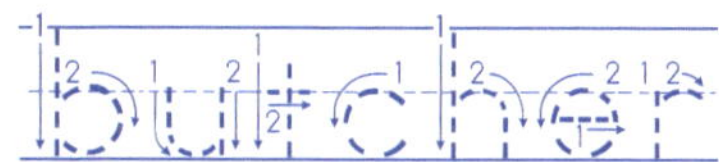 

pharmacist

Farmasøyt

That Pharmacist saved a person's life.

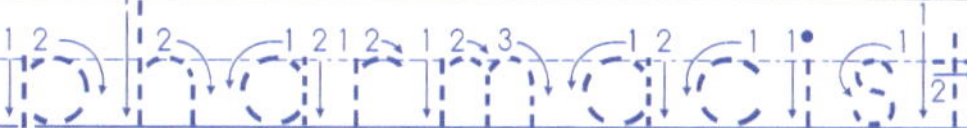

receptionist

Resepsjonist

He is a Receptionist.

politician

Politiker

He wants to be a Politician.

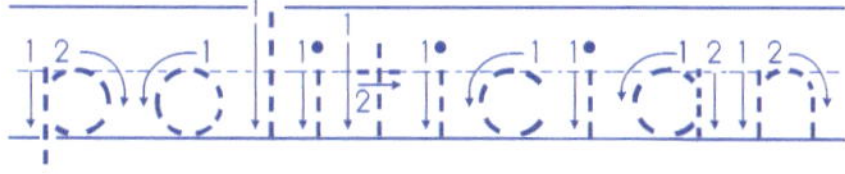 

tour guide

Tur guide

That Tour guide led us around Japan.

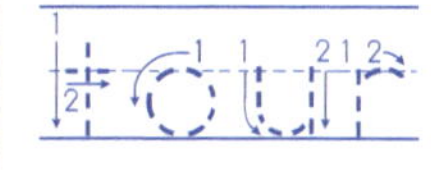 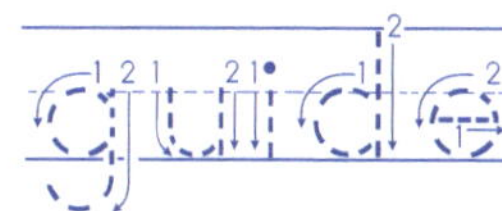 

entrepreneur

entreprenør

He is an Entrepreneur.

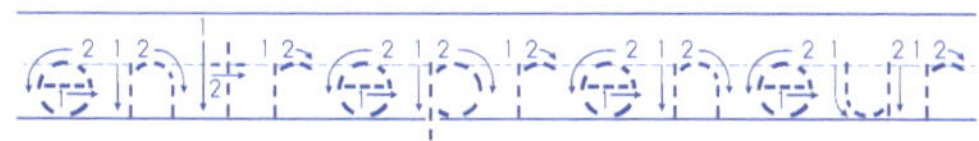 

ballet dancer

Ballettdanser

She is training to be a Ballet dancer.

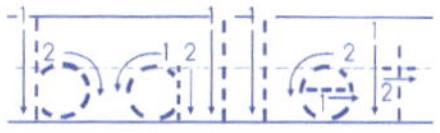 

astronaut

Astronaut

He is a great astronaut.

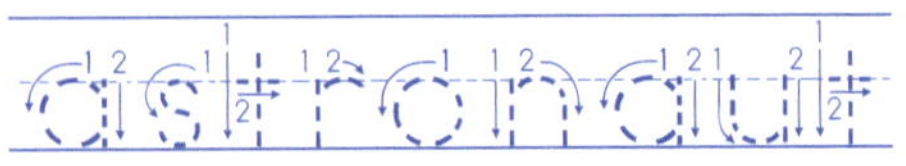 

judge

Dømme

That Judge is always fair.

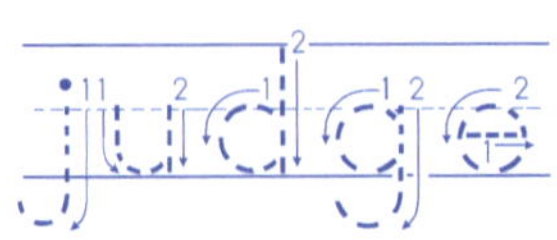 

lawyer

Advokat

The lawyer is serious.

cashier

Kasserer

She is a cashier at the market.

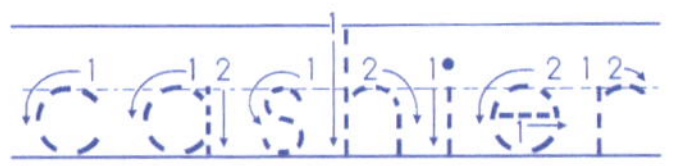 

taxi driver

Drosjesjåfør

He is a fast Taxi driver.

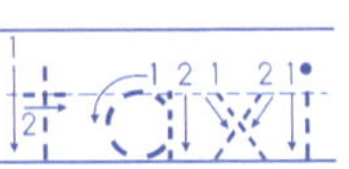 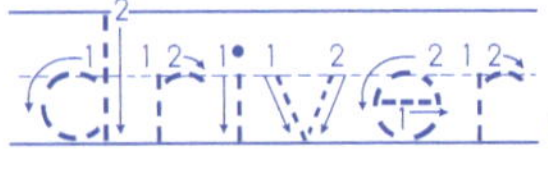 

plumber

Rørlegger

That Plumber fixes toilets.

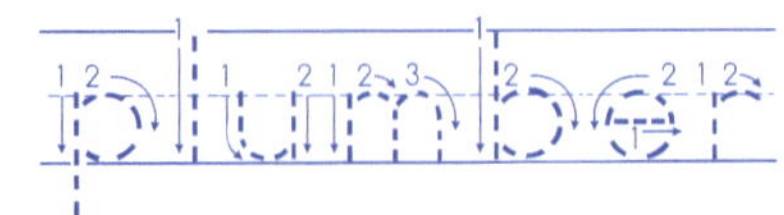 

musician

Musiker

She wants to be a Musician like her teacher.

 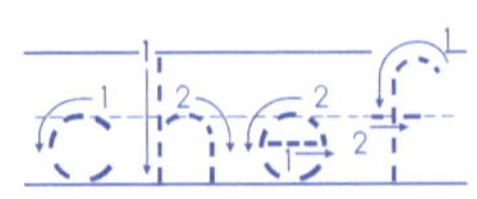

chef

Chef

The chef makes fast food.

baker

Baker

That baker is a bread.

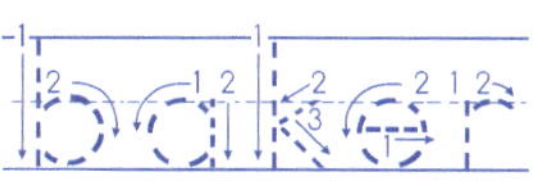

artist

kunstner

That Artist came from Italy.

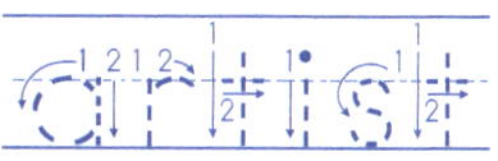

actor

Skuespiller

That actor is famous.

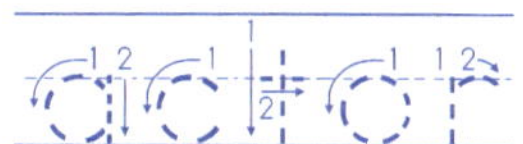

bartender

barkeeper

The Bartender works in a bar.

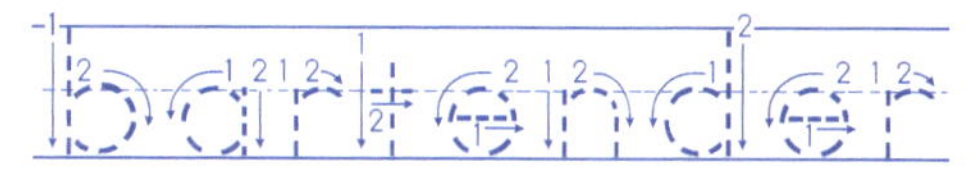

hairdresser

Frisør

That girl is a Hairdresser.

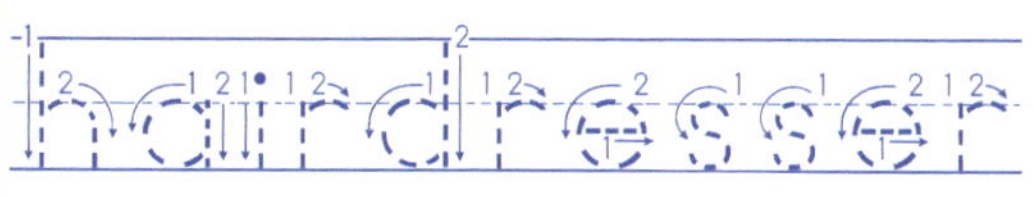

bishop

Bishops

He is a Bishop.

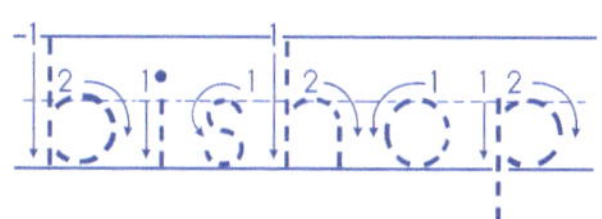

optician

Optiker

She went to an Optician.

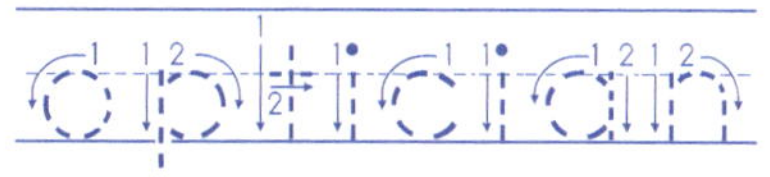

florist

Florist

She is a great Florist.

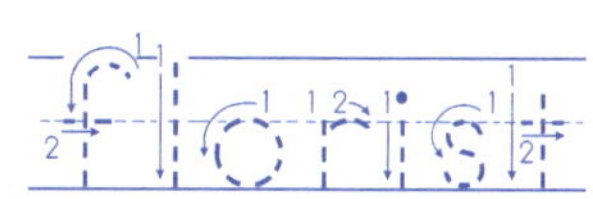

writer
Forfatter

He is a famous author.

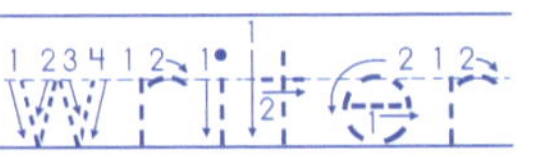

accountant
Regnskapsfører

My accountant is loyal.

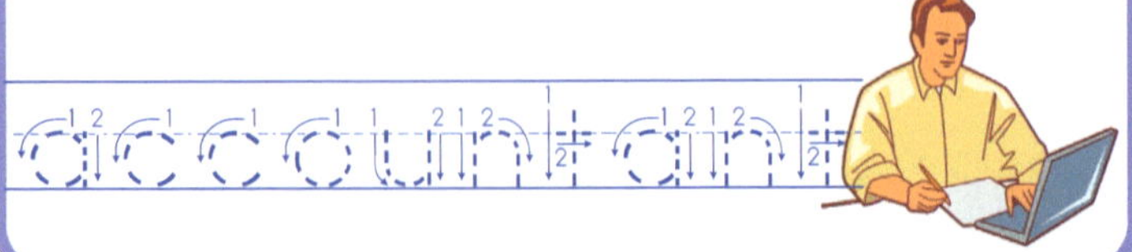

wine
Vin

That wine tastes good.

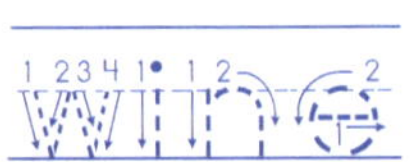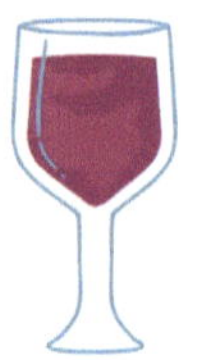

coffee
Kaffe

That coffee is bitter.

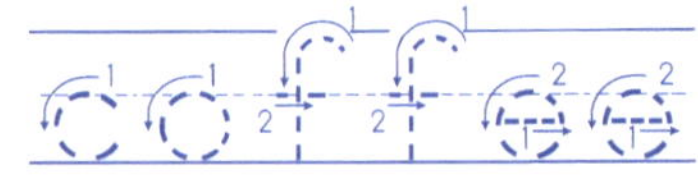

lemonade
Limonade

The lemonade is refreshing.

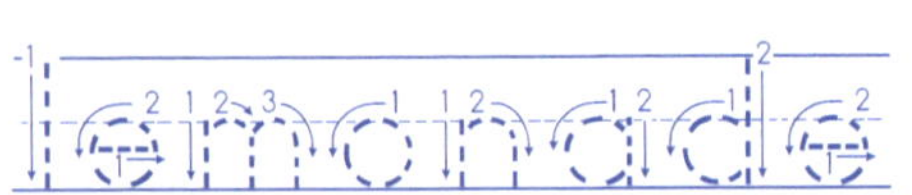

hot chocolate
Varm sjokolade

I drink hot chocolate every day.

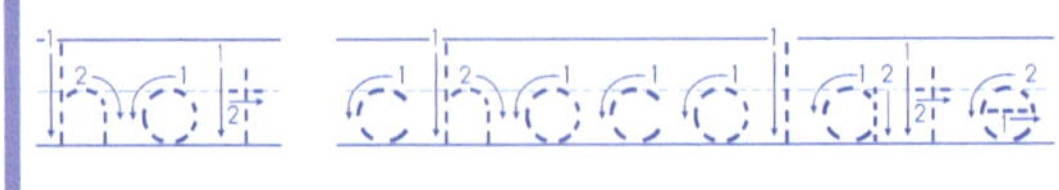

milkshake
Milkshake

The milkshake has whipped cream.

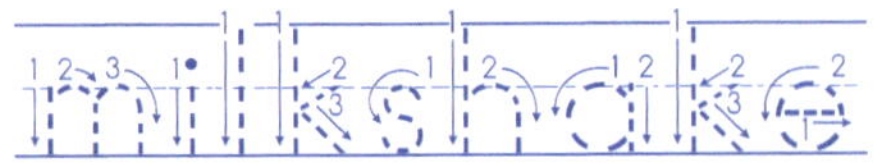

water
Vann

The water is not cold.

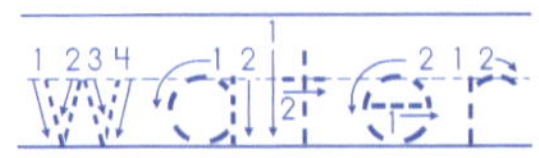

tea

Te

The tea is hot.

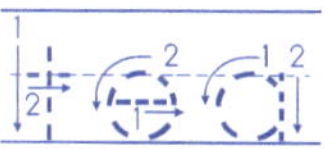

milk

Melk

Milk is white.

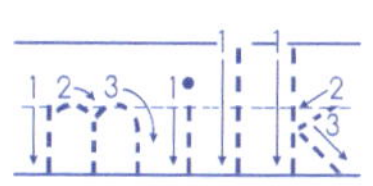

beer

Øl

The beer is foamy.

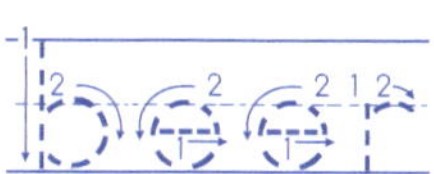

soda

Soda

The soda is fizzy.

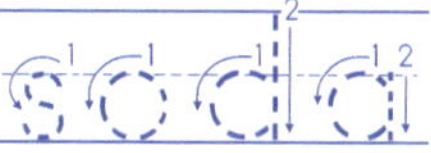

smoothie

Smoothie

The smoothie is a watermelon flavor.

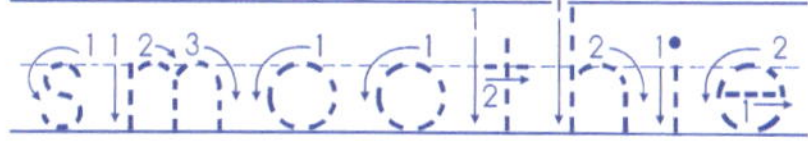

milkshake

Milkshake

The milkshake has whipped cream.

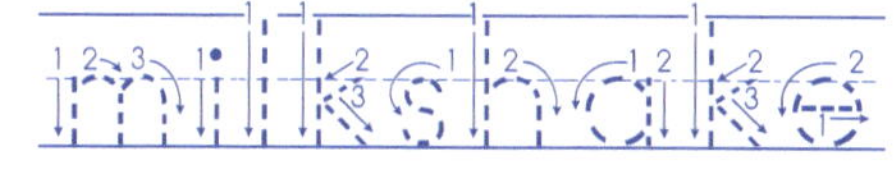

coconut milk

Kokosnøttmelk

The coconut milk is yummy.

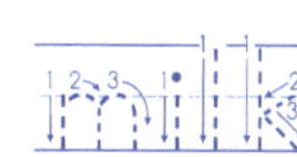

orange juice

appelsinjuice

The orange juice is made from oranges.

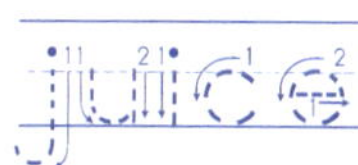

cocoa

kakao

The cocoa is sweet.

cheese

Ost

The cheese is creamy.

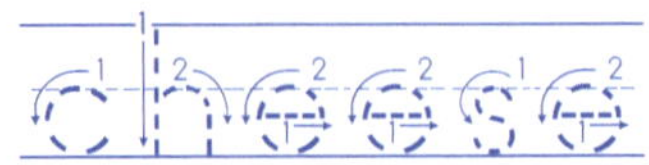 

egg

Egg

The egg is fried.

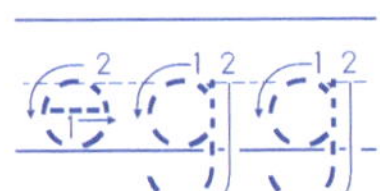 

butter

Smør

The butter is put on bread.

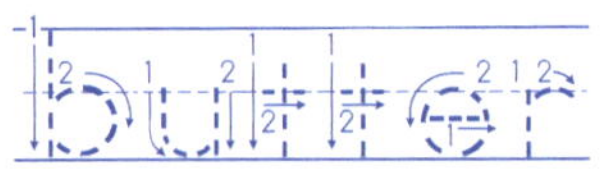 

margarine

margarin

Margarine looks like butter.

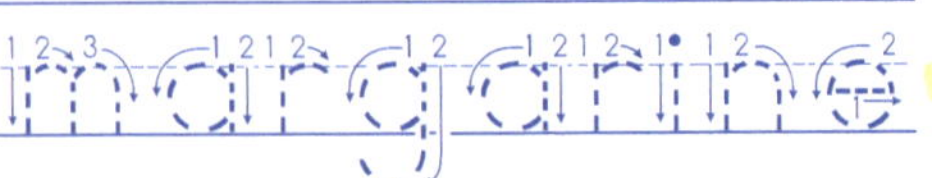 

yogurt

Yoghurt

That yogurt is popular.

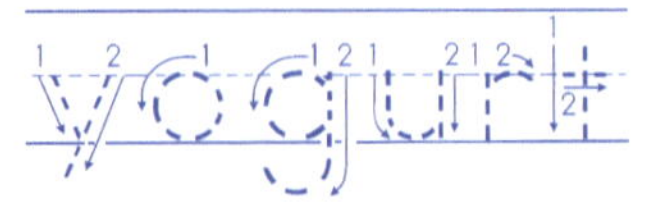 

cottage cheese

Kesam

The cottage cheese is put on crackers.

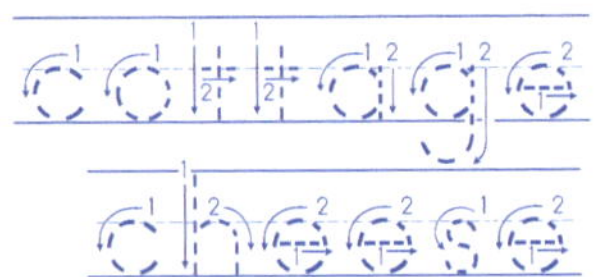  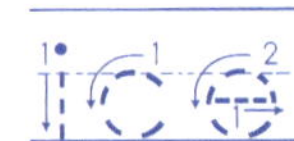

ice cream

Iskrem

They have a triple scoop of ice cream.

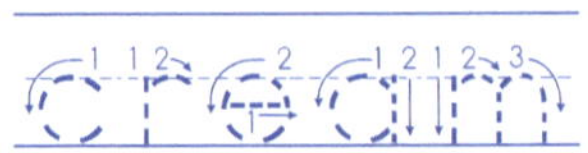 

cream

Krem

That is a lot of creams.

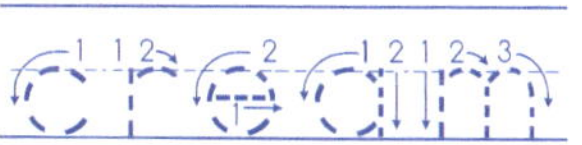

sandwich

Smørbrød

That sandwich is healthy.

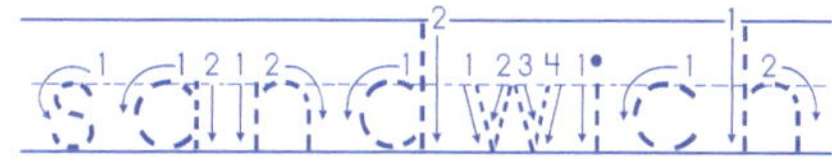

sausage

Pølse

Americans love sausages.

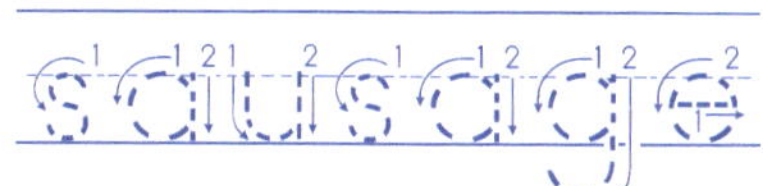

hamburger

hamburger

That hamburger looks happy.

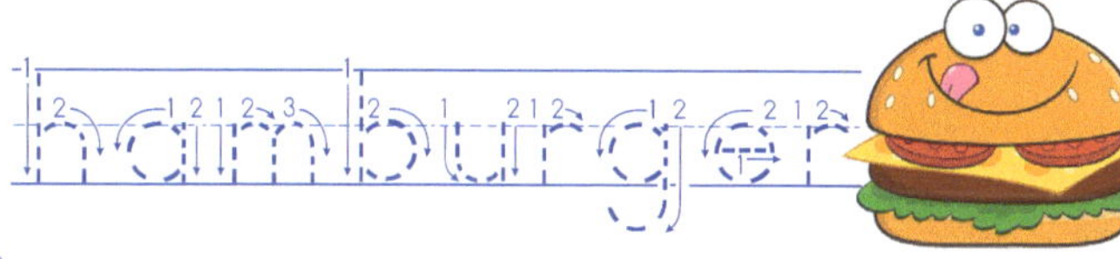

hot dog

Pølse

That hot dog has mustard on it.

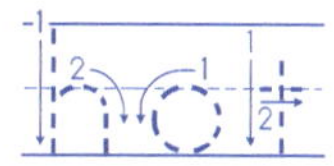
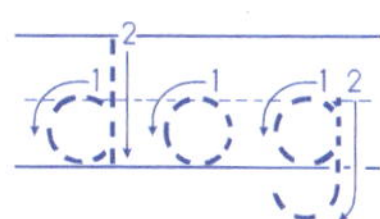

bread

Brød

That bread is saying hello.

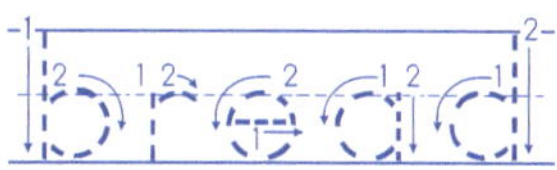

pizza

pizza

That pizza is cheesy.

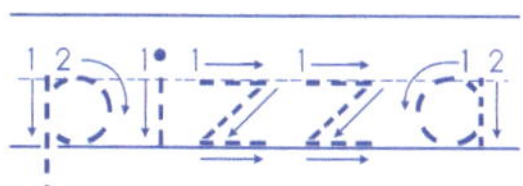

steak

biff

We grilled the steak.

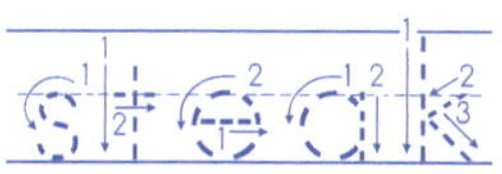
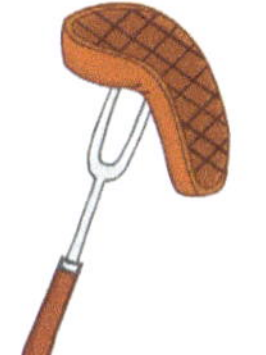

roast chicken

Stekt kylling

Roast Chicken is delicious.

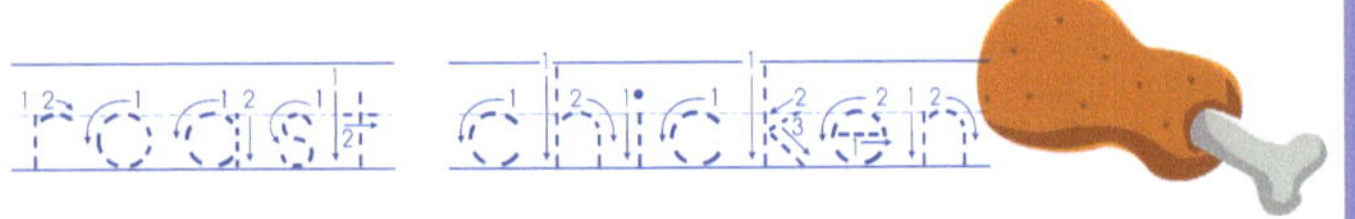

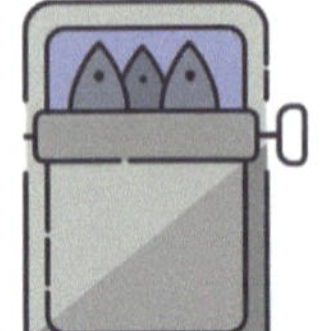

fish

Fisk

You can buy canned fish in the market.

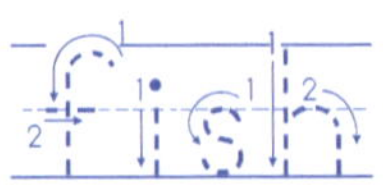

seafood

Sjømat

Lobster is expensive seafood.

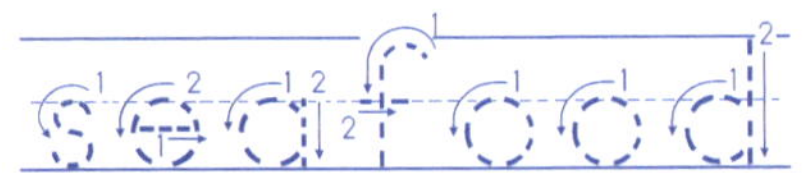

ham

Skinke

He put hams in the sandwiches.

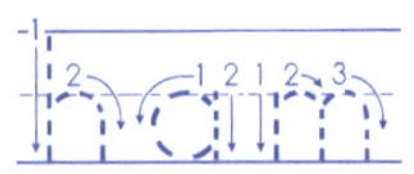

kebab

kebab

Kebab is a delicacy in America.

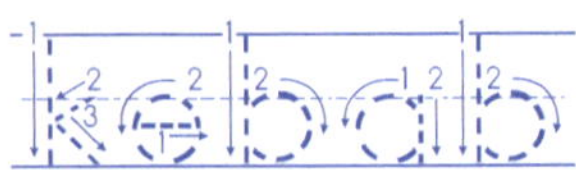

bacon

Bacon

That bacon is smiling.

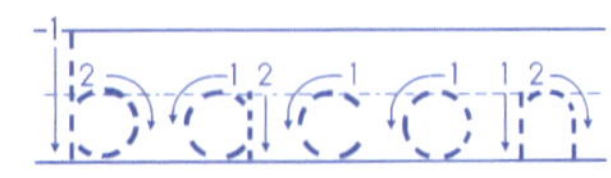

sour cream

Rømme

You can dip your chips in sour cream.

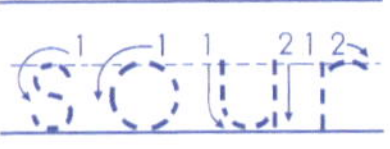

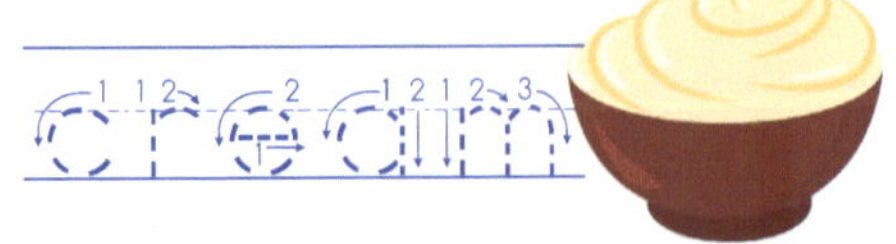

cow

Ku

Cows are black and white.

rabbit

Kanin

That rabbit is fun to play with.

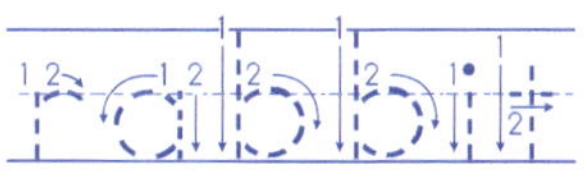 

duck

And

That duck is content.

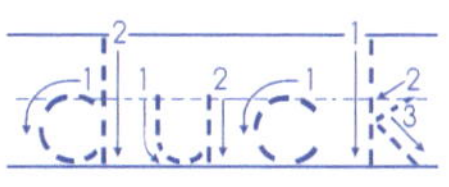 

shrimp

Reke

The shrimp has six legs.

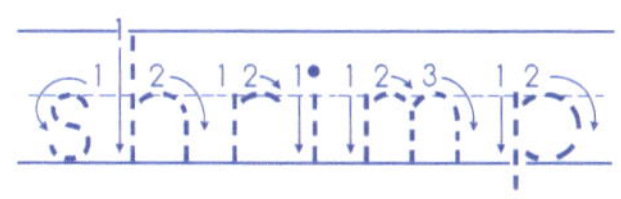 

pig

Gris

That pig is pink and fat.

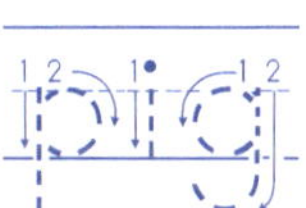 

bee

Bie

The bee has a stinger.

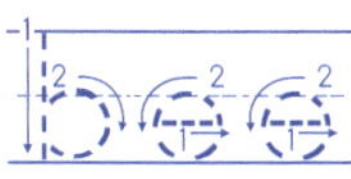 

goat

Geit

That goat has a white horn.

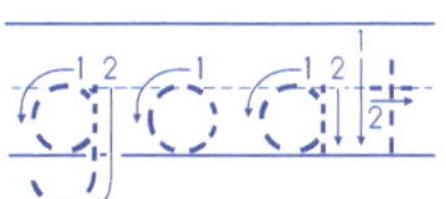 

crab

Krabbe

The crab has two big pincers.

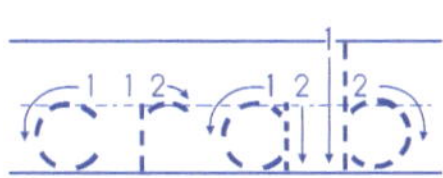 

deer

Hjort

That deer is sleeping.

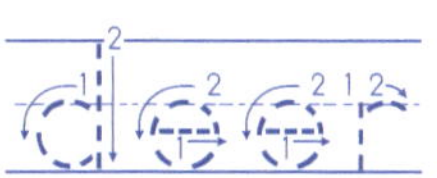 

turkey

Tyrkia

The turkey has a giant tail.

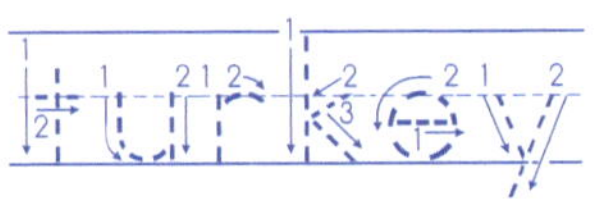

dove

Due

That dove is carrying a plant.

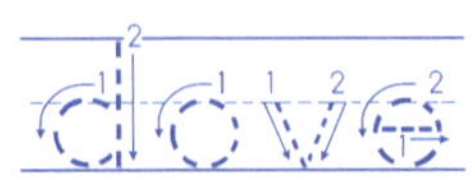

sheep

Sau

That sheep has fluffy wool.

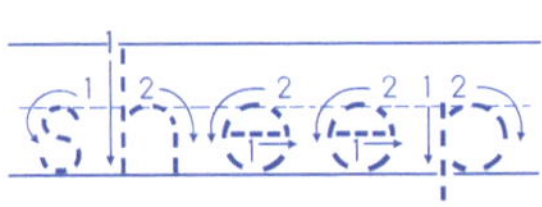

fish

Fisk

That fish has colorful fins.

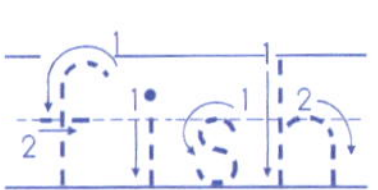

chicken

Kylling

That chicken is waking everybody up.

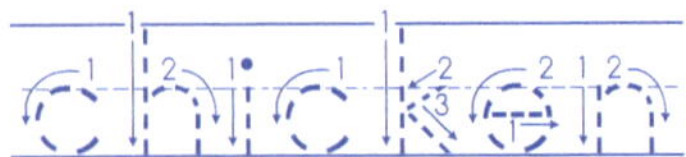

horse

Hest

The horse has a red mane.

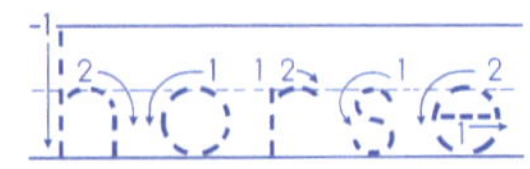

wing chair

stol

That wing chair is yellow.

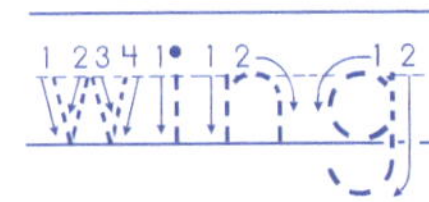

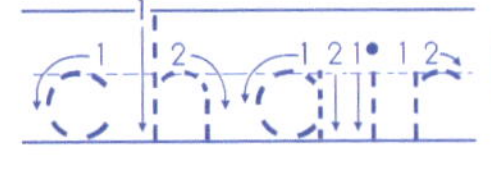

tv stand

TV-benk

The TV stand can hold books.

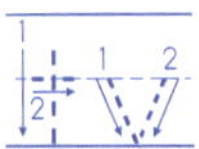

sofa

Sofa

The sofa is comfortable to sit on.

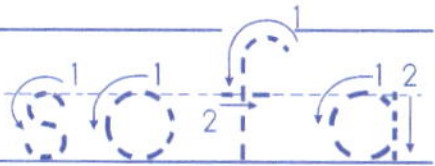 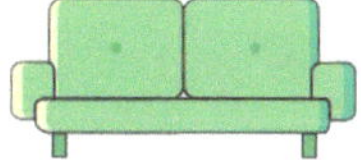

cushion

puter

The cushion helps soften your seat.

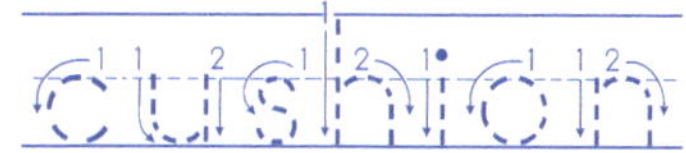 

telephone

Telefon

The telephone is ringing.

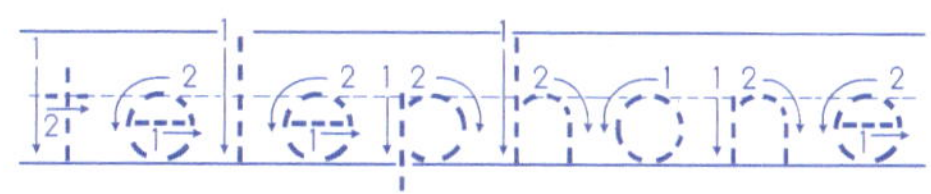 

television

Fjernsyn

That television is big.

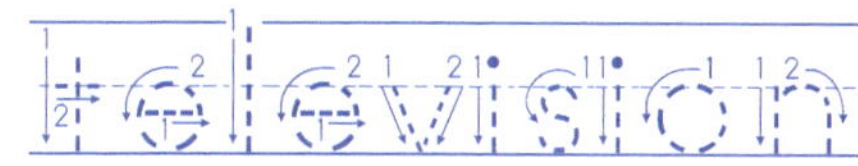 

speaker

Høyttalere

That speaker is used to increase the volume.

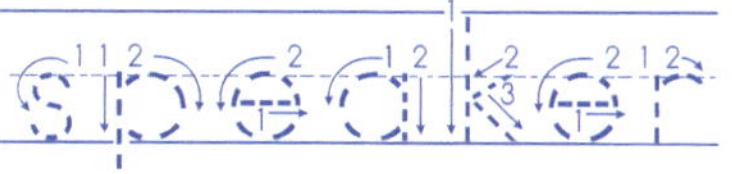 

end table

sidebord

That end table is sparkling clean.

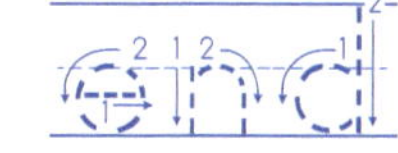 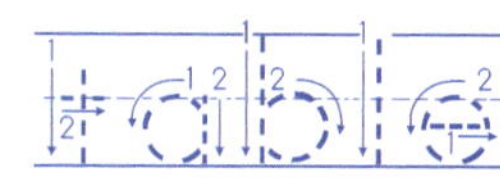 

tea set

Tesett

That tea set is from China.

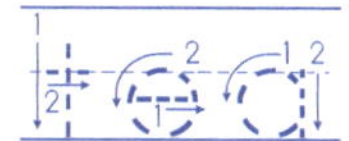 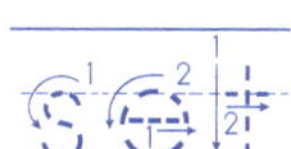 

fireplace

Peis

The fireplace makes me warm.

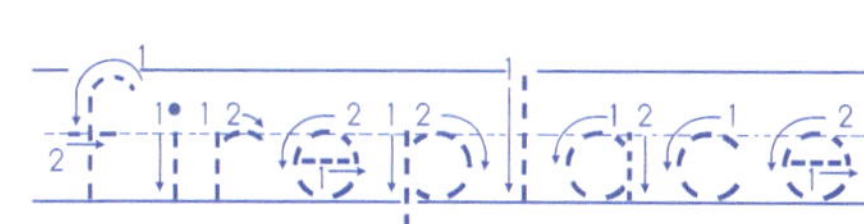 

remote

fjernkontroller

The remote has lots of buttons.

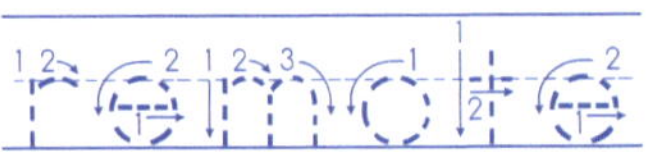 

fan

elektrisk vifte

The fan is blowing wind.

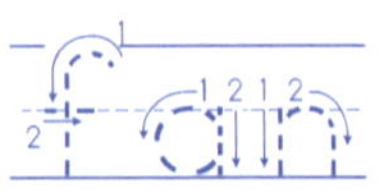 

floor lamp

Gulv lampe

The floor lamp is very tall.

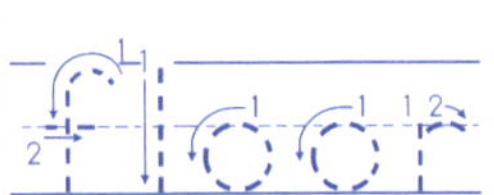 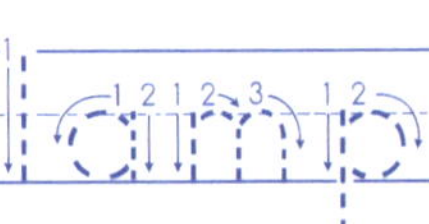 

carpet

Teppe

The carpet is soft and silky.

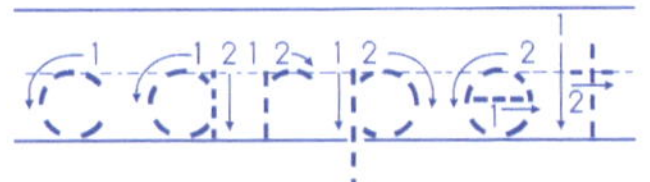 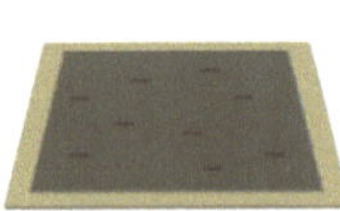

table

skrivebord

The table is made of wood.

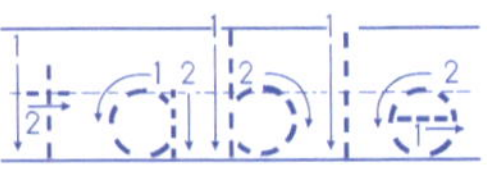 

blinds

blinds

I will pull the blinds down.

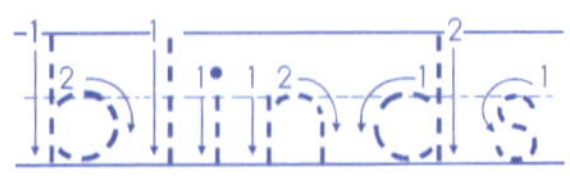 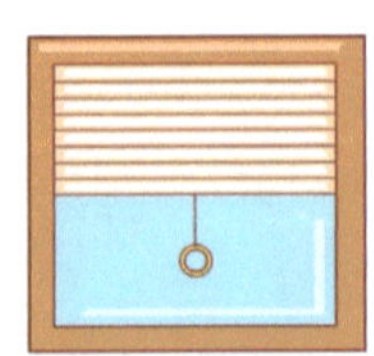

curtains

gardiner

She opened the curtains.

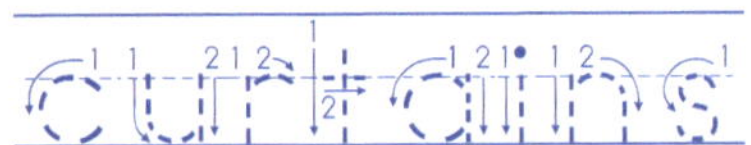 

picture

Bilde

The picture is about the mountains and the sky.

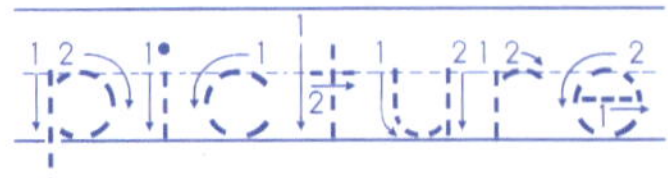 

vase

Vase

The roses are all in a vase.

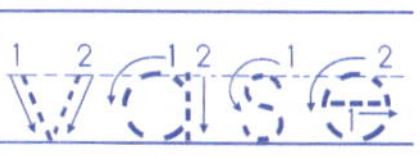 

clock

Klokke

The alarm clock is beeping.

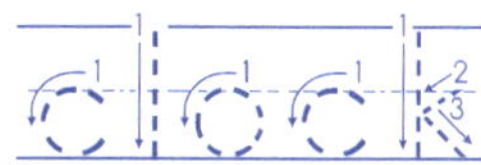 

pillow

Pute

The pillow is pink and yellow.

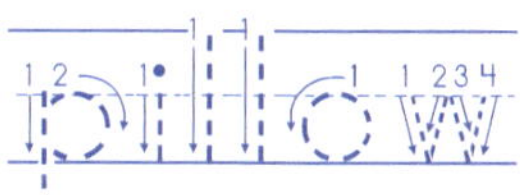 

hat stand

lue henger

The hat stand has only one hat on it.

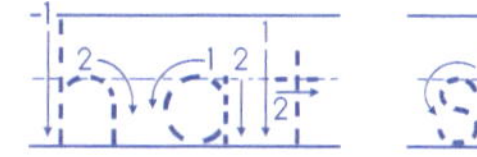  

dressing table

Sminkebord

I have made up on my dressing table.

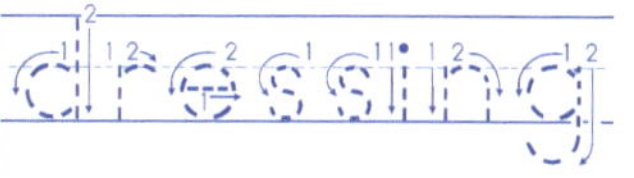 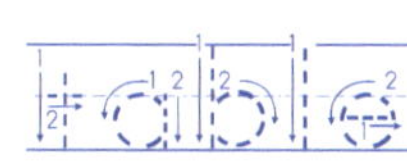 

table lamp

Bordlampe

The table lamp will help me see in the dark.

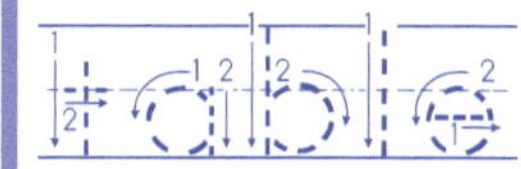 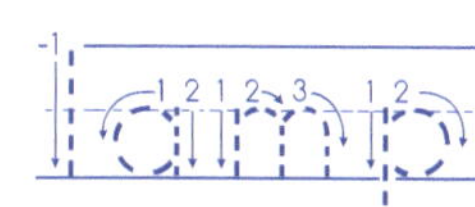 

mirror

Speil

The mirror is very tall.

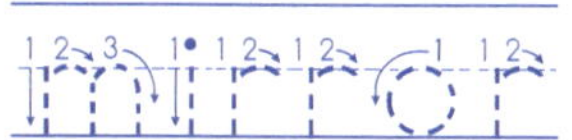 

ironing board

Strykebrett

Please don't touch the ironing board; it's hot!

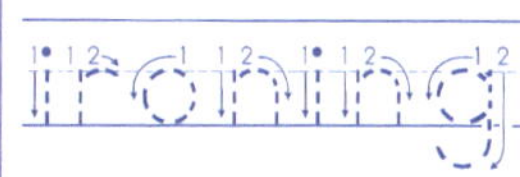  

hope chest

eske med skuff

You can keep your clothes in the hope chest.

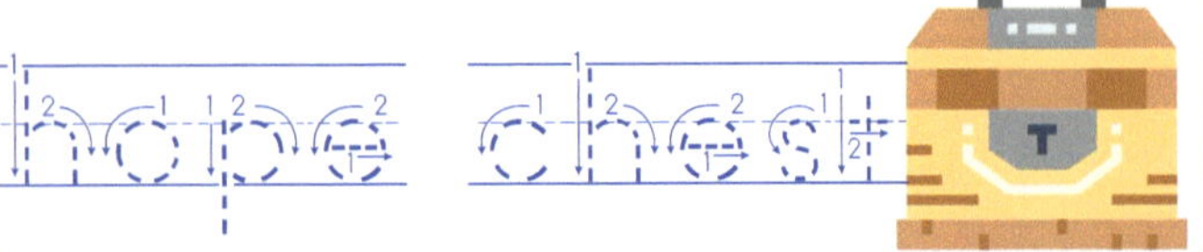

night table

nattbord

The night table has my lamp on it.

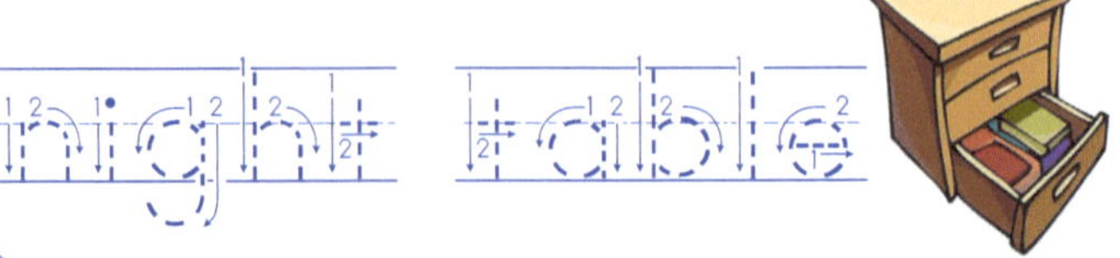

bed

seng

The bed is charming.

air-conditioner

Klimaanlegg

The air conditioner is cold.

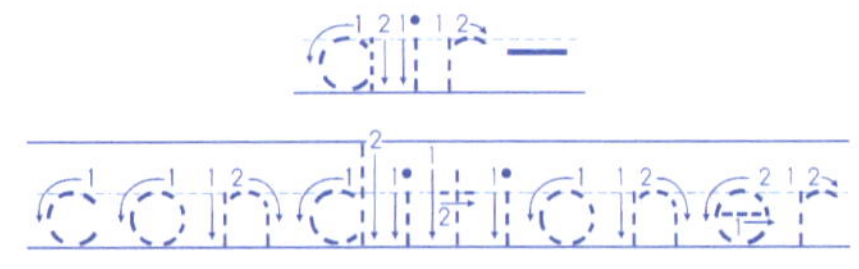
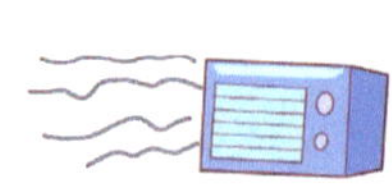

jug

mugge

The measuring jug has nothing inside.

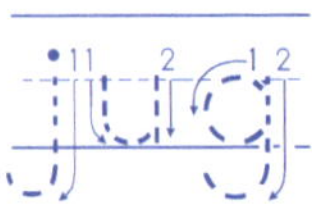

toothpaste

Tannkrem

The toothpaste is mint flavored.

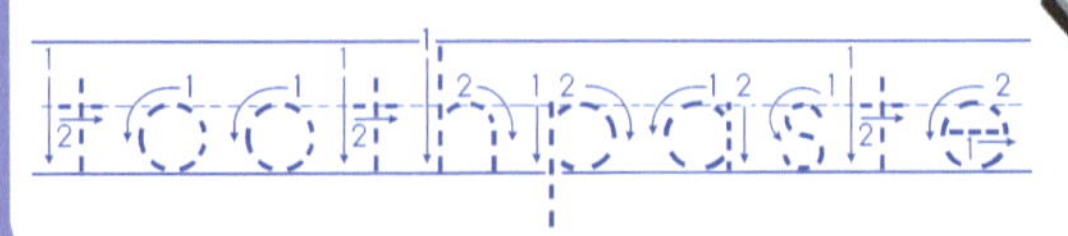
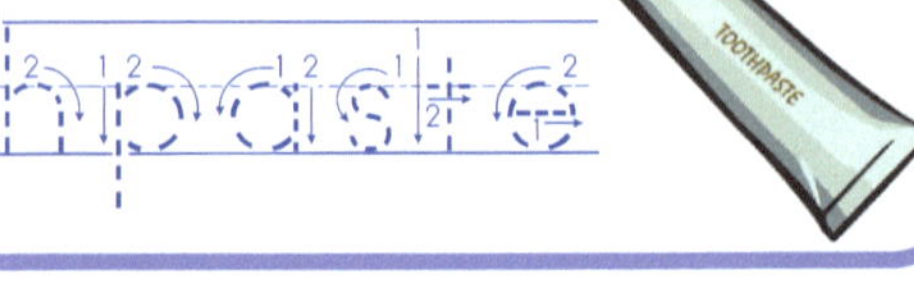

toothbrush

Tannbørste

The toothbrush has toothpaste on it.

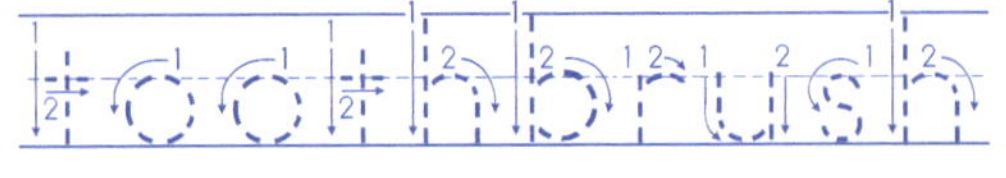

soap

Såpe

The soap is very bubbly.

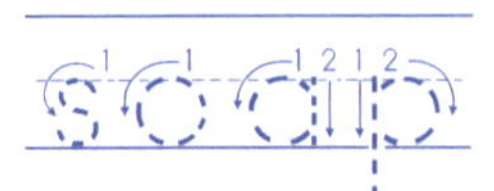
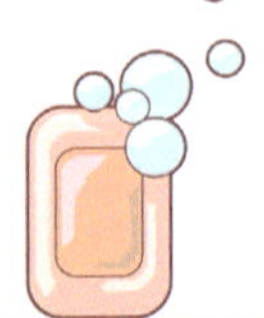

clothespin

Klesklype

The clothespin will clip my clothes.

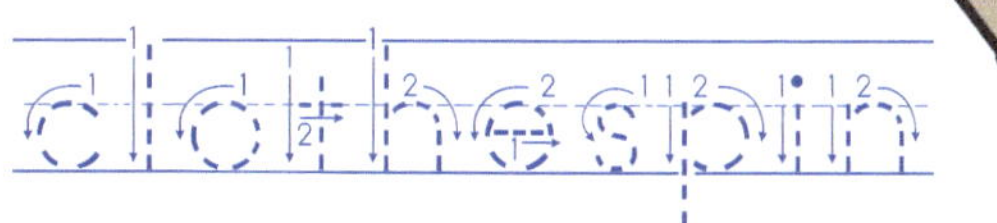 

hanger

Hanger

The hanger is hanging my boots.

 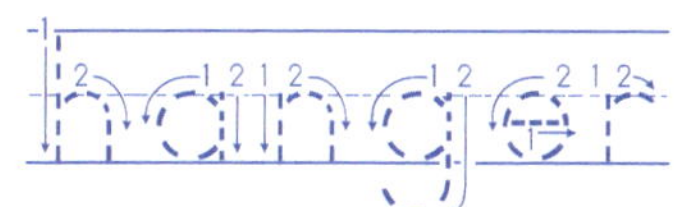

hair dryer

Hårføner

The hair dryer will blow my hair.

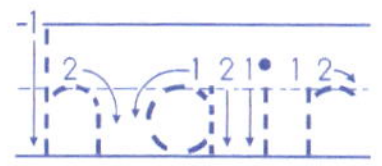 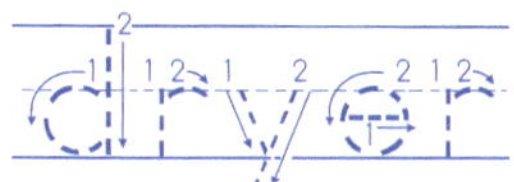 

shampoo

Sjampo

The shampoo is used to clean your hair.

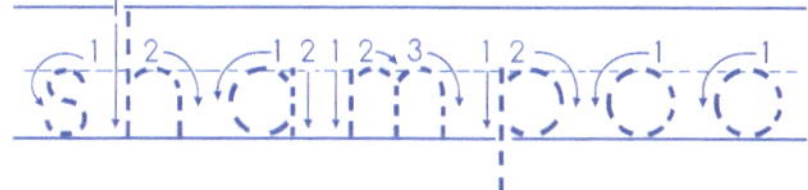 

bubble

Boble

The bubbles are amusing to play in.

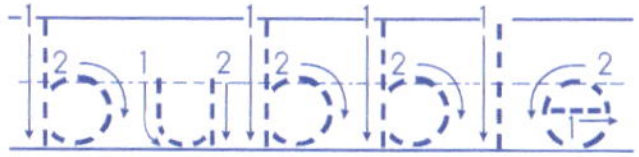 

brush

Børste

She is brushing her hair with the brush.

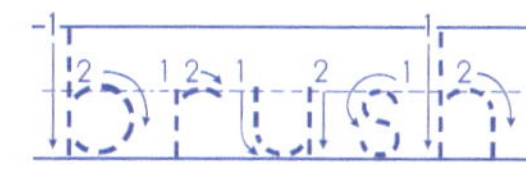 

toilet paper

Toalettpapir

The toilet paper is used to dry your hands.

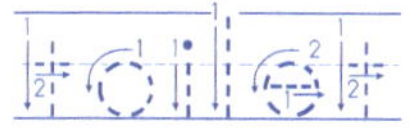 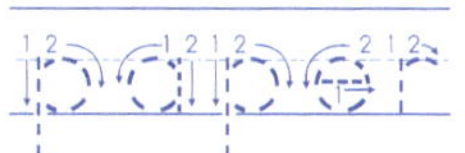 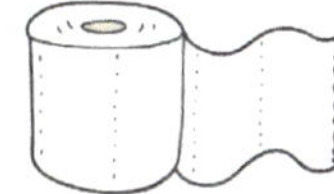

towel

Håndkle

We have two towels on the rack.

 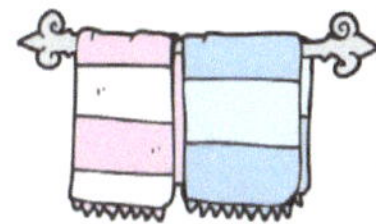

clothesline

klessnor

My shirt is hanging on the clothesline.

shower

Dusj

The shower is spraying water.

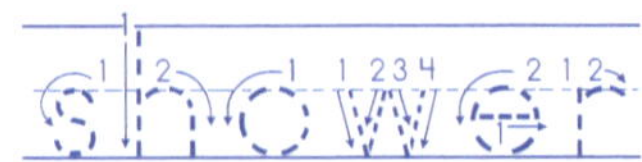 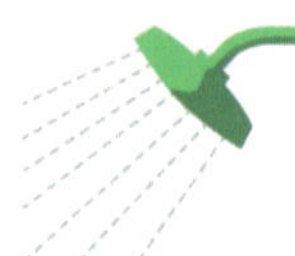

bathtub

Badekar

The bathtub is comfortable.

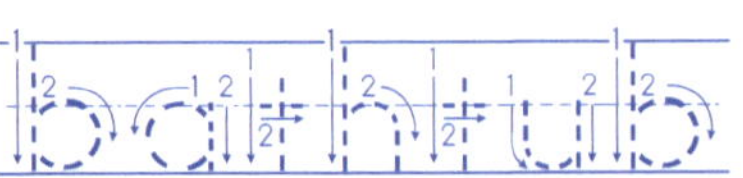 

laundry detergent

Vaskemiddel

The laundry detergent is used with the washing machine.

bucket

Bøtte

Can you help me fill up the bucket?

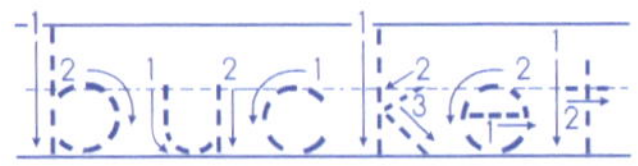

mops

Mops

The mop is used for mopping the floor.

 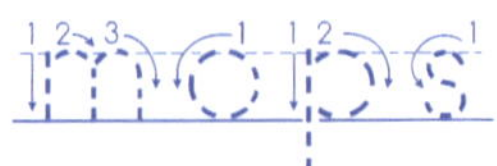 

liquid soap

Flytende såpe

I use liquid soap to wash my hands.

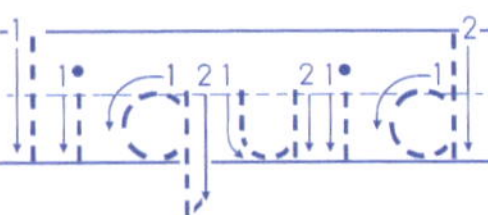 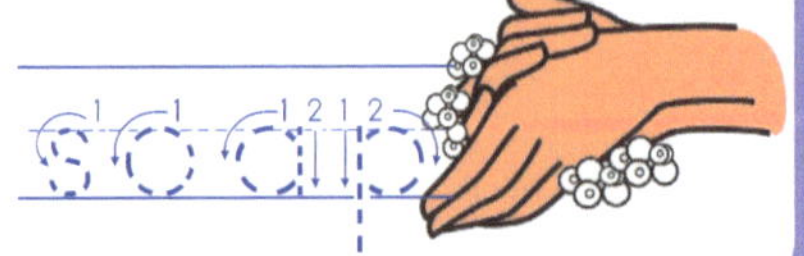

washing powder

Vaskepulver

I will scoop up the washing powder.

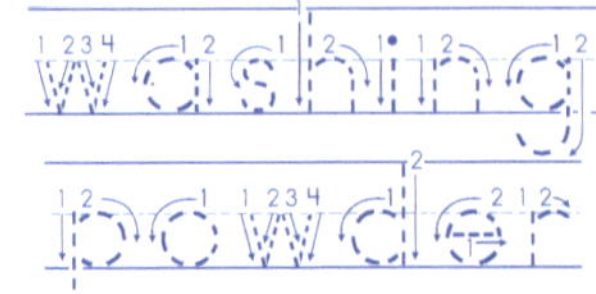 

trash bag

Søppelsekk

The trash bag is full of trash.

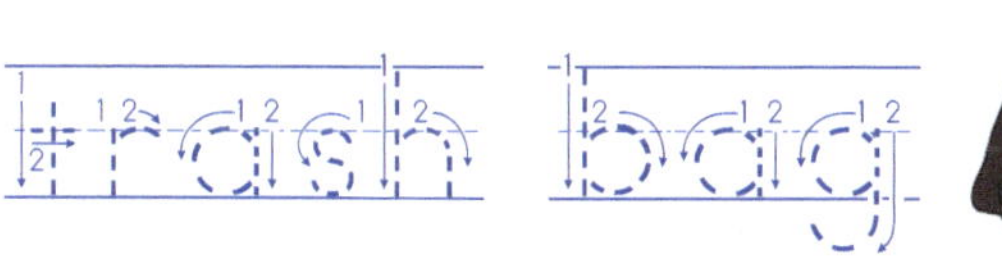  

trash can

Søppelbøtte

You have only to put recycle the trash in the trash can.

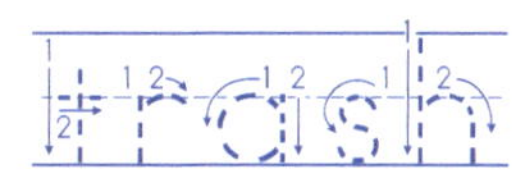 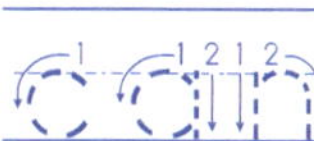

sinks

vasker

It will help if you wash your hands in the sink.

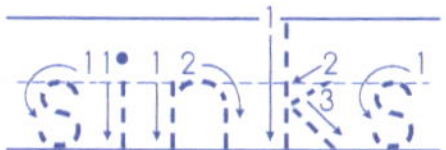

toilet bowl

Doskål

She let her bunny use the toilet.

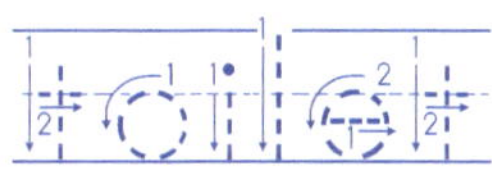 

washing machine

Vaskemaskin

The washing machine is where you wash your clothes.

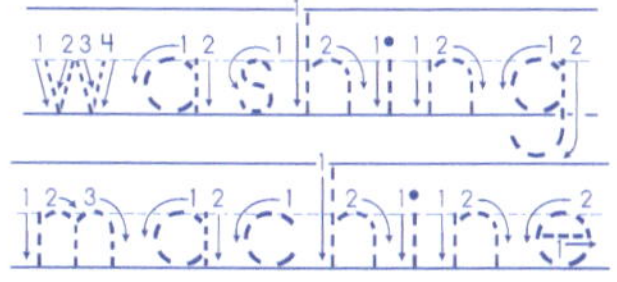

laundry basket

Skittentøyskurv

She is putting all the clothes into the laundry basket.

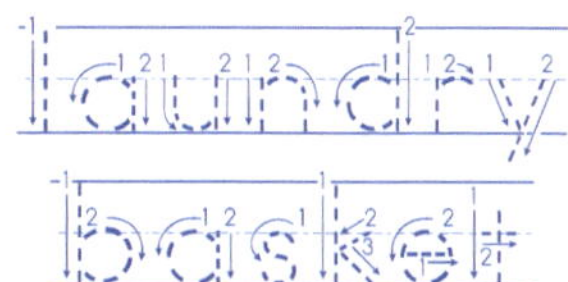 

razor

Barberhøvel

He uses the razor to shave his beard.

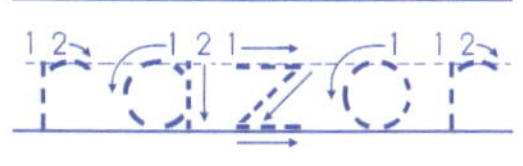

electric razor

elektrisk barbermaskin

The electric razor works faster than the normal one.

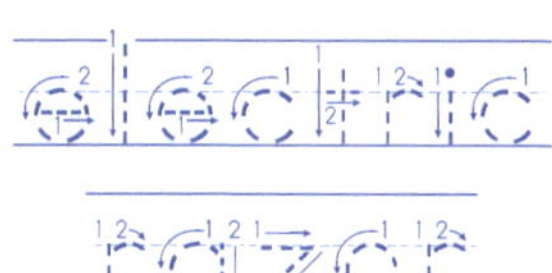 

shaving cream

Barberkrem

The shaving cream is fluffy.

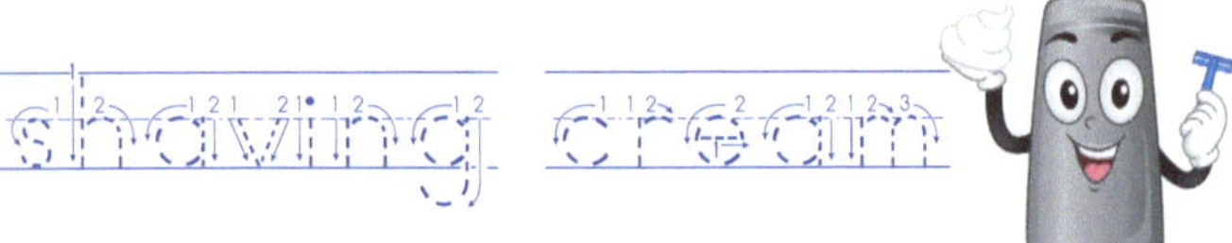 

mouthwash

Munnvann

The mouthwash smells very nice.

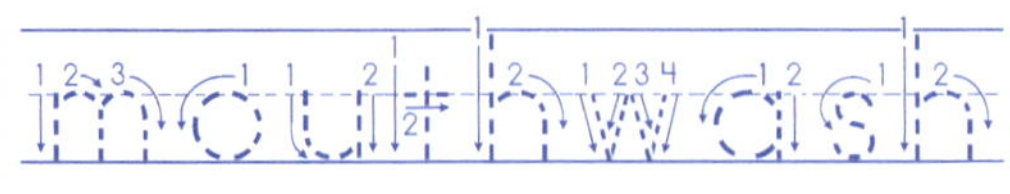

cotton bud

bomullsdott

We use Q-tip for many things.

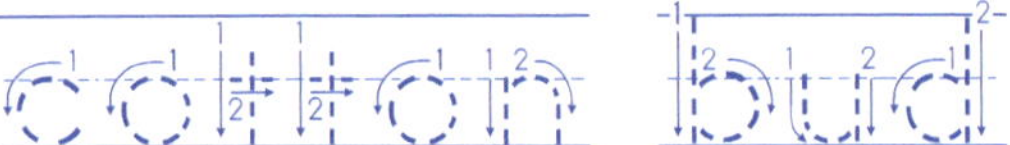 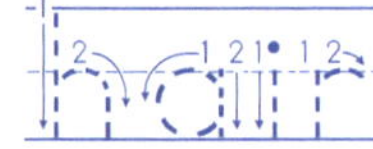

hair brush

Hårbørste

She brushes her hair with her hair brush.

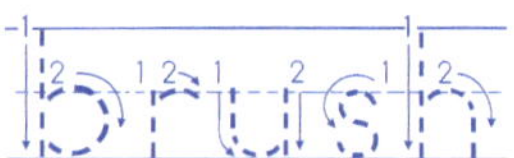 

comb

Kam

Her dad will comb her hair for her.

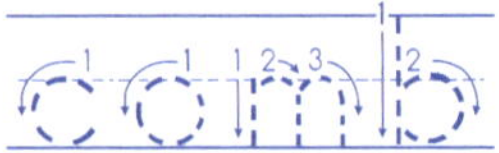 

cleanser

cleanser

Put the cap back on the cleanser bottle.

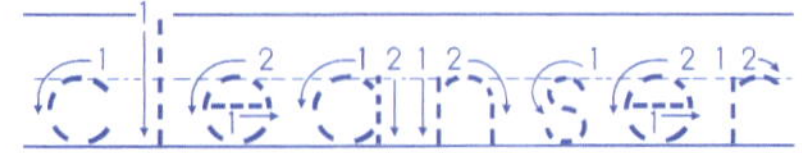 

scale

Scale

You can measure things on a scale.

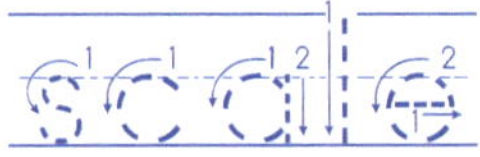 

tissue paper

Tørkepapir

The tissue is on the counter.

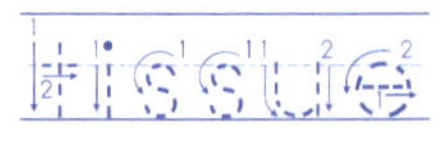 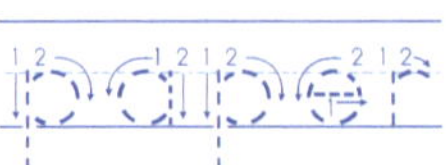 

bath toys

Badeleker

The little duck is a bath toy.

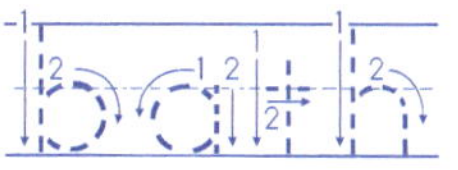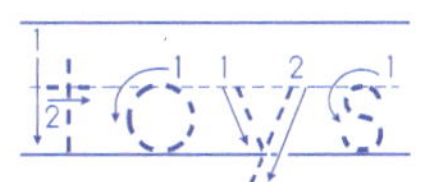

faucet

Kran

The faucet is broken.

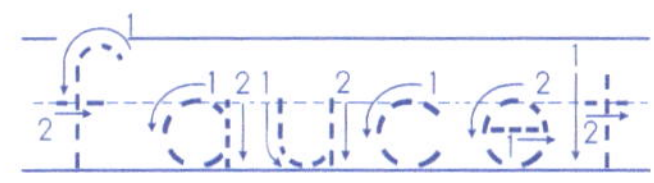

mirror

Speil

He is looking in the mirror.

bath mat

Baderomsteppe

The bath mat is purple and yellow.

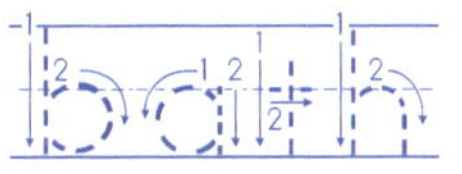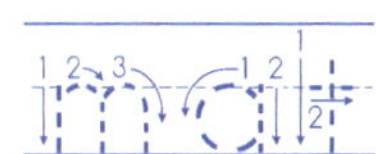